RECORDED VERSIONS
GUITAR

AUTHENTIC TRANSCRIPTIONS
WITH NOTES AND TABLATURE

RAY LAMONTAGNE

TILL THE SUN TURNS BLACK

Music transcriptions by Pete Billmann

ISBN-13: 978-1-4234-2639-4
ISBN-10: 1-4234-2639-8

HAL•LEONARD®
CORPORATION

7777 W. BLUEMOUND RD. P.O. BOX 13819 MILWAUKEE, WI 53213

Visit Hal Leonard Online at
www.halleonard.com

Be Here Now

Words and Music by Ray LaMontagne

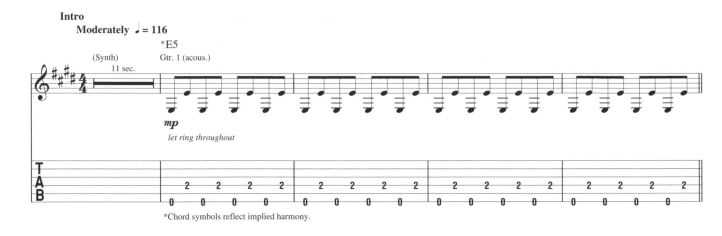

Intro
Moderately ♩ = 116

*Chord symbols reflect implied harmony.

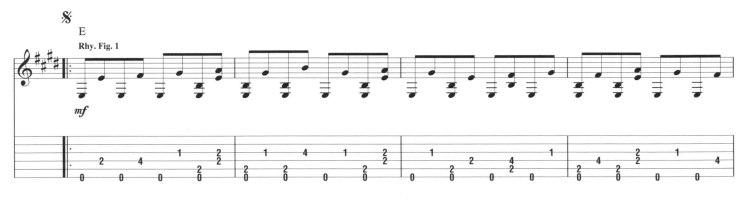

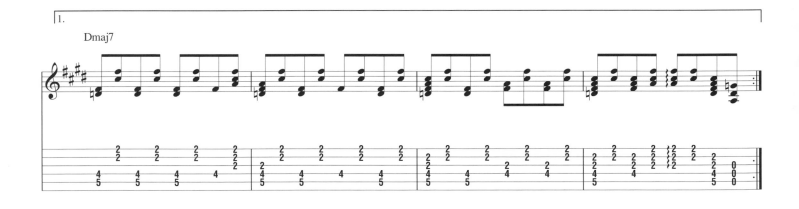

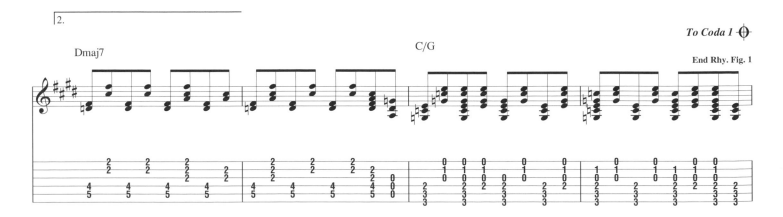

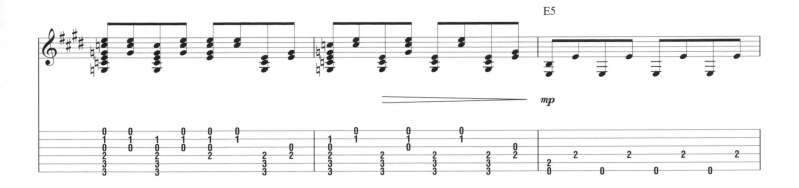

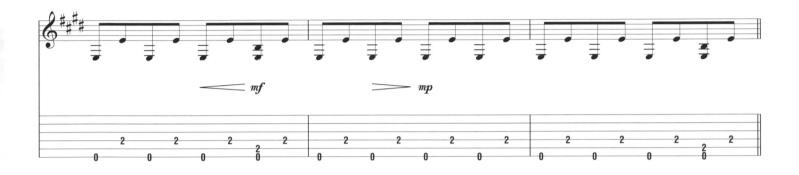

𝄋𝄋 Verse

Gtr. 1: w/ Rhy. Fig. 1

1. Don't let your mind ___ get wea-ry and ___ con- fuse ___ your will. ___
2. Don't let your soul ___ get lone- ly, child. ___ It's on- ly time, ___
3. Don't lose your faith ___ in me ___ and I ___ will try ___ not to ___

___ Be still, ___ don't ___ try. ___
___ it will ___ go ___ by. ___
___ lose faith ___ in you. ___

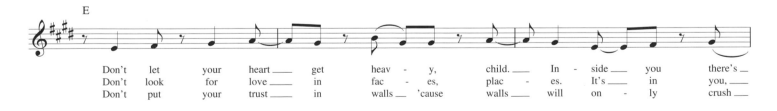

Don't let your heart ___ get heav- y, child. ___ In- side ___ you there's ___
Don't look for love ___ in fac- es, plac- es. It's ___ in you, ___
Don't put your trust ___ in walls ___ 'cause walls ___ will on- ly crush ___

___ a strength that lies, ___   lies.
___ that's where ___ you'll ___ find ___   kind '- ness.
___ you when ___ they ___ fall.

5

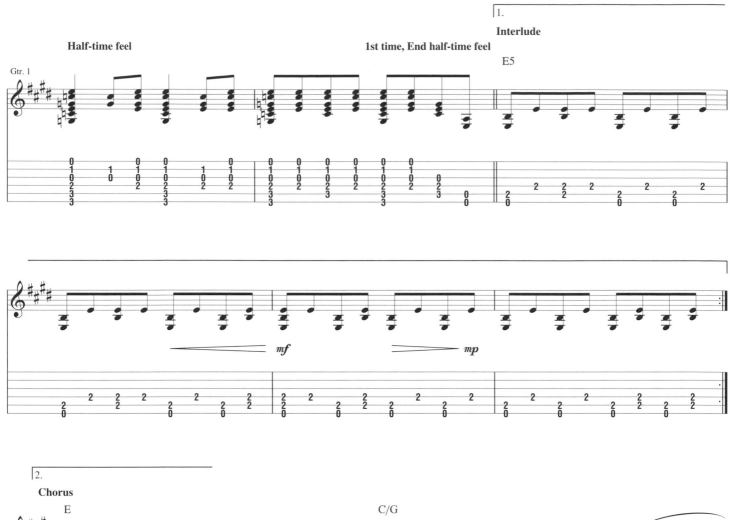

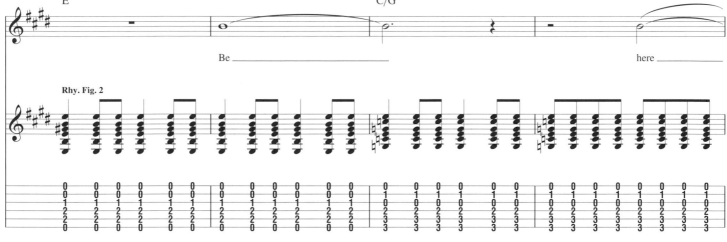

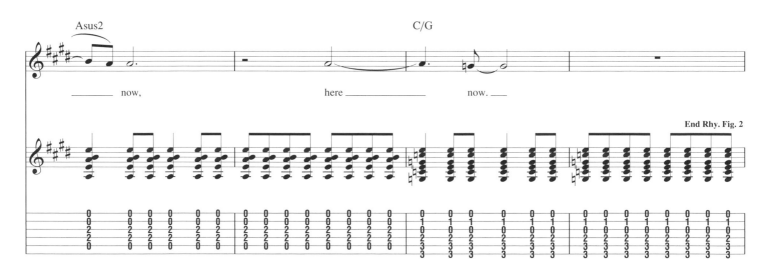

Be _____ here _____

now, here _____ now. _____

To Coda 2 $\oplus$

Interlude

End half-time feel

Gtr. 1

D.S. al Coda 1
(take repeat)

mf *mp*

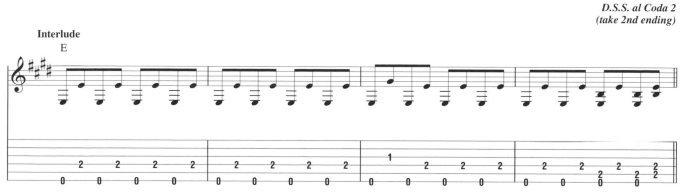

$\oplus$ **Coda 1**

D.S.S. al Coda 2
(take 2nd ending)

Interlude

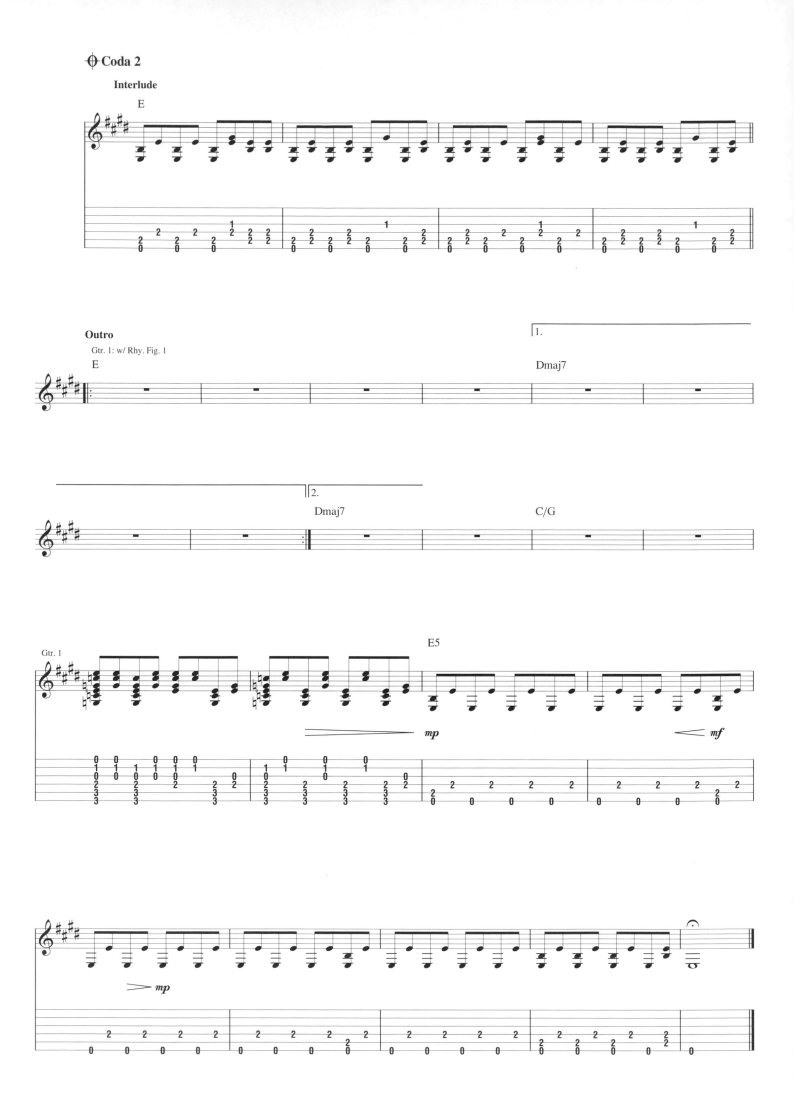

Empty

Words and Music by Ray LaMontagne

Gtr. 1: Capo II

Intro
Moderately fast ♩ = 163

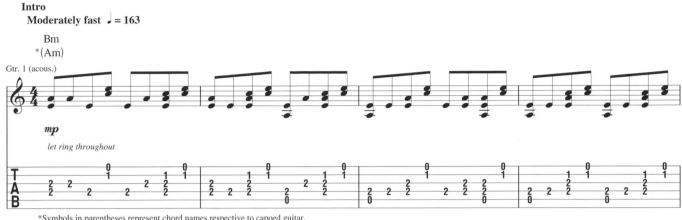

*Symbols in parentheses represent chord names respective to capoed guitar.
 Symbols above reflect actual sounding chords. Capoed fret is "0" in tab.
 Chord symbols reflect implied harmony.

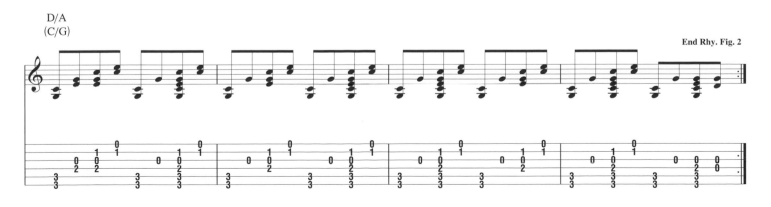

hard some - how to let go of my _____ pain.
__ me with that coun - try mouth __ so _____ plain.
__ al - read - y dead __ that walk be - side _____ me.
Out -
There's a

Gtr. 1: w/ Rhy. Fig. 3

side the rain __ is tap - ping on ___ the leaves. _____ To me it sounds
lot of things _ I don't un - der - stand, why so man - y peo - ple lie. _____

On past the bust - ed back __ of that old and rust - ed

Cad - il - lac ___ that sinks ___ in - to ___ this field col - lect - ing ___
__ like they're ap - plaud - ing us, ___ the qui - et love ___ we've ___
__ It's the hurt ___ I hide ___ that fuels the fire in -

Chorus

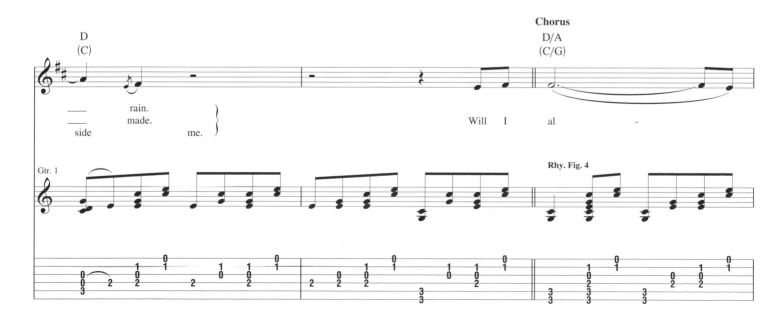

__ rain.
__ made.
side me.
Will I al -

Gtr. 1

Rhy. Fig. 4

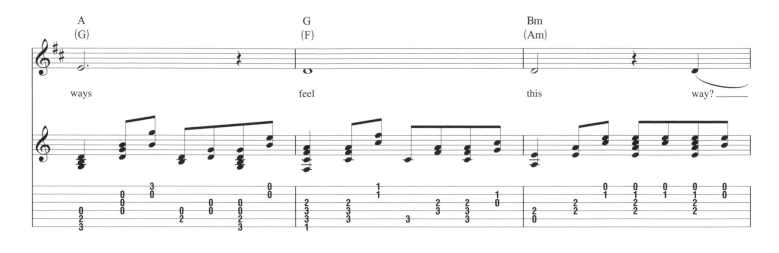

ways   feel   this   way? _____

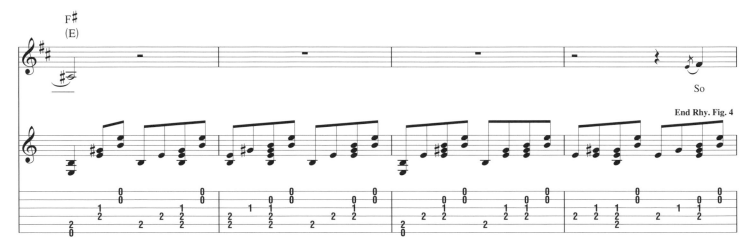

So

End Rhy. Fig. 4

To Coda ⊕

1st & 2nd times, Gtr. 1: w/ Rhy. Fig. 4
3rd time, Gtr. 1: w/ Rhy. Fig. 4 (1st 6 meas.)

emp - ty, _____   so   es - tranged. ___

1.

Interlude
Gtr. 1: w/ Rhy. Fig. 1
Bm
(Am)

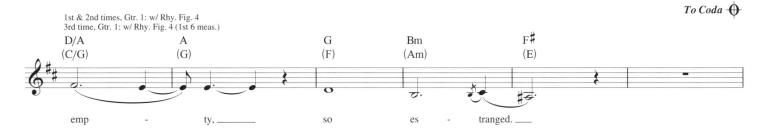

2. (And) of these cut -

2.

Viola & Cello Solo
Gtr. 1: w/ Rhy. Fig. 2 (2 times)
G
(F)

*Gtr. 2

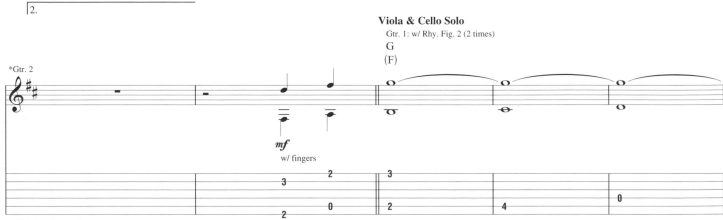

mf
w/ fingers

*Viola & cello arr. for gtr.

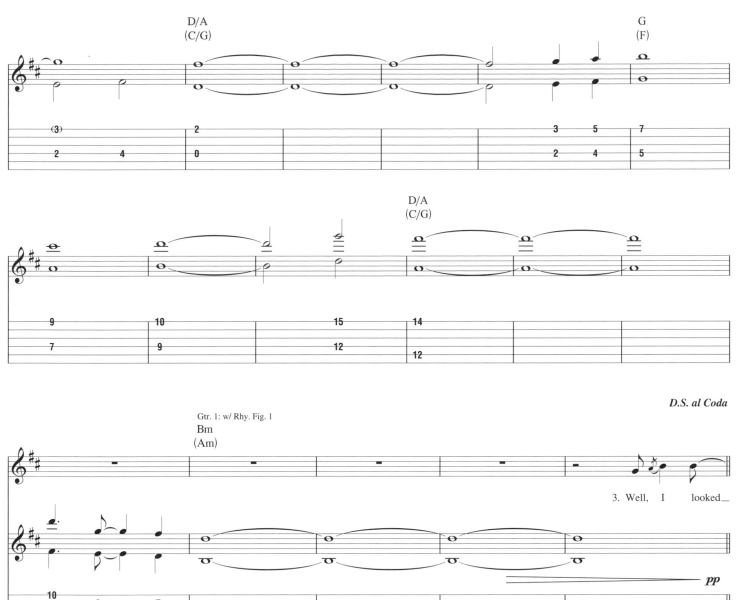

D.S. al Coda

Gtr. 1: w/ Rhy. Fig. 1

3. Well, I looked

pp

Barfly

Words and Music by Ray LaMontagne

Intro
Moderately ♩ = 82

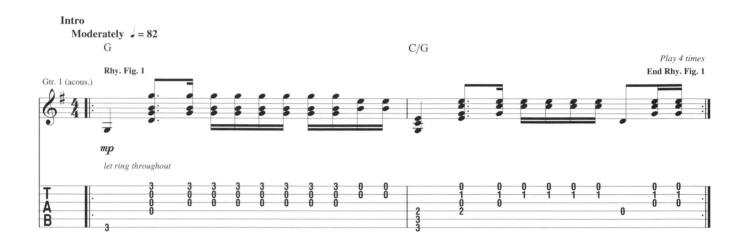

Verse

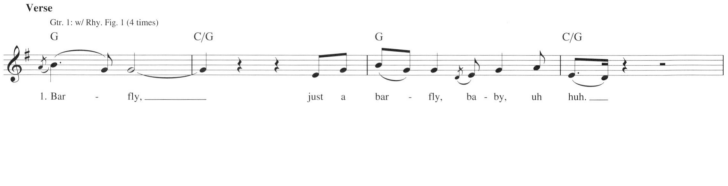

1. Bar - fly, _____ just a bar - fly, ba - by, uh huh. _____

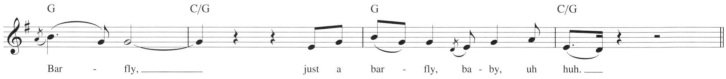

Bar - fly, _____ just a bar - fly, ba - by, uh huh. _____

Chorus

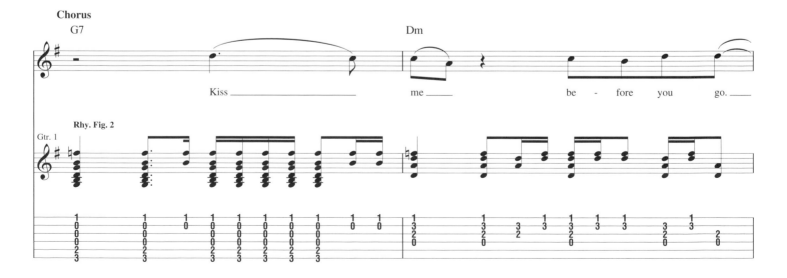

Kiss _____ me _____ be - fore you go. _____

I'm go - in' no - where late - ly. _____

End Rhy. Fig. 2

Interlude

Gtr. 1: w/ Rhy. Fig. 1 (2 times)

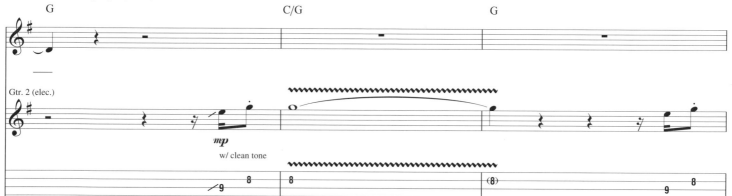

Gtr. 2 (elec.)

mp

w/ clean tone

Verse

Gtr. 1: w/ Rhy. Fig. 1 (8 times)   Gtr. 2 tacet

2. Bar - fly, _____ a bar - fly, ba - by, uh

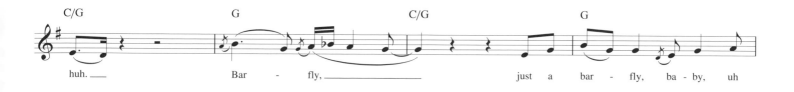

huh. ___ Bar - fly, _____ just a bar - fly, ba - by, uh

huh. ___ Slow ___ down. ___ Slow down, you move too fast. ___

Slow _____ down. _____

Slow down, you move too fast. _____

Chorus

Kiss _____ me _____ be - fore you go. _____

I'm go - in' no - where late - ly.

Gtr. 1: w/ Rhy. Fig. 2

Kiss _____ me _____ be - fore you go. _____ I'm go - in' no -

Interlude

Gtr. 1: w/ Rhy. Fig. 1

Whispered:
- where late - ly.

I'm go - in' no -

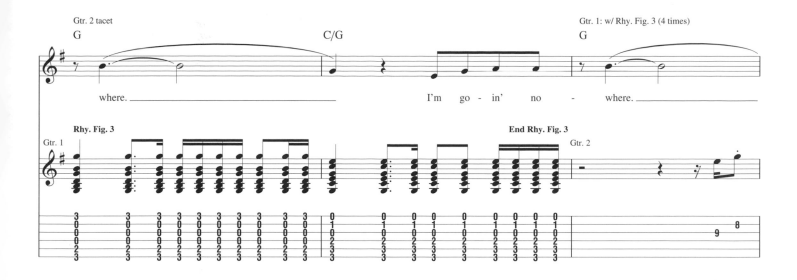

where. _____ I'm go - in' no - where. _____

____ I'm go - in' no - where. ____ I'm go - in' no - where.

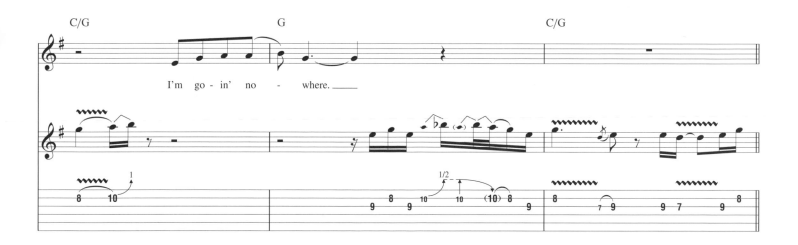

I'm go - in' no - where. ____

Outro-Guitar Solo

Gtr. 1: w/ Rhy. Fig. 1 (8 times)

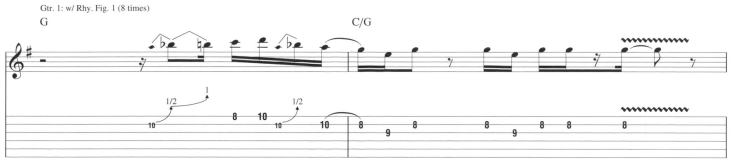

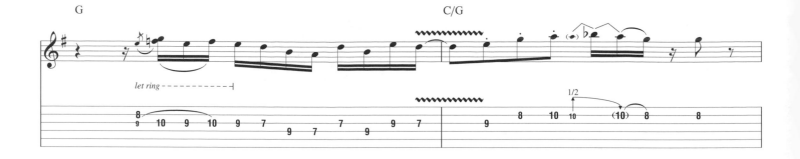

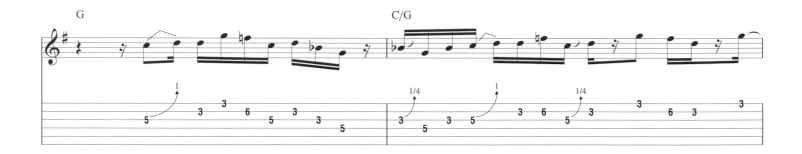

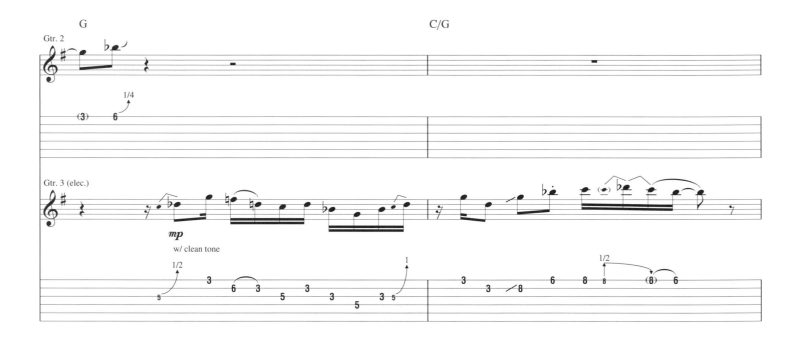

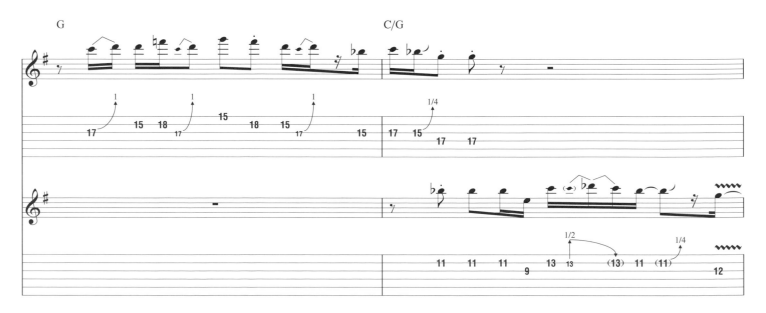

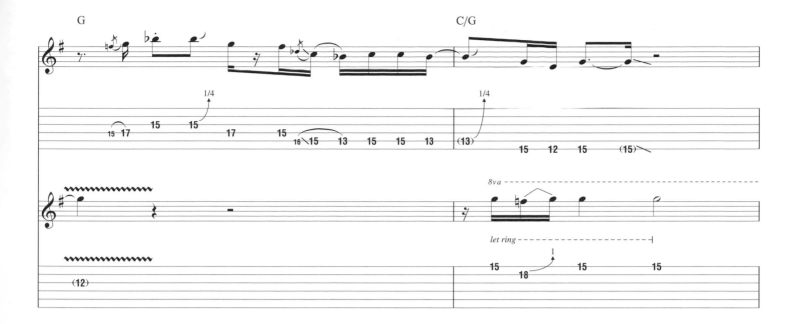

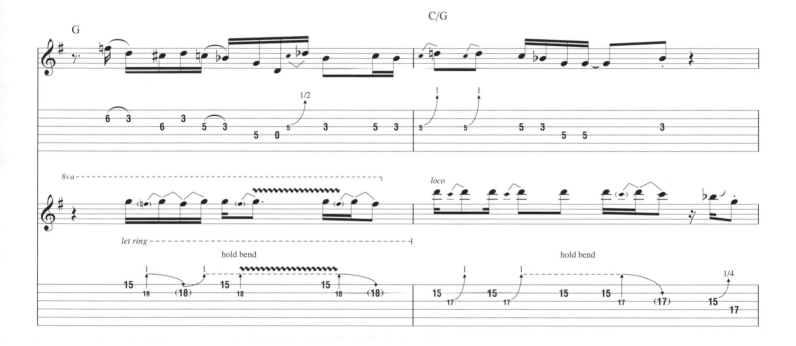

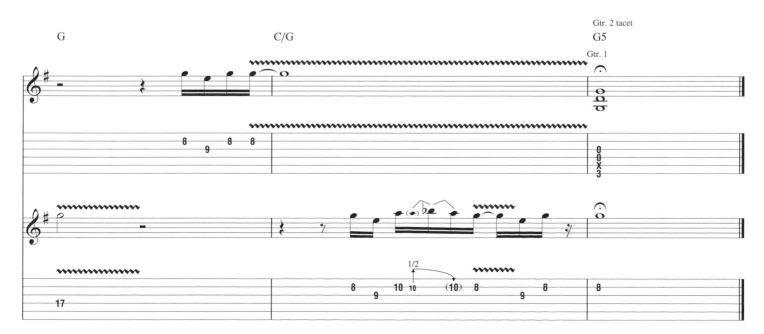

Three More Days

Words and Music by Ray LaMontagne

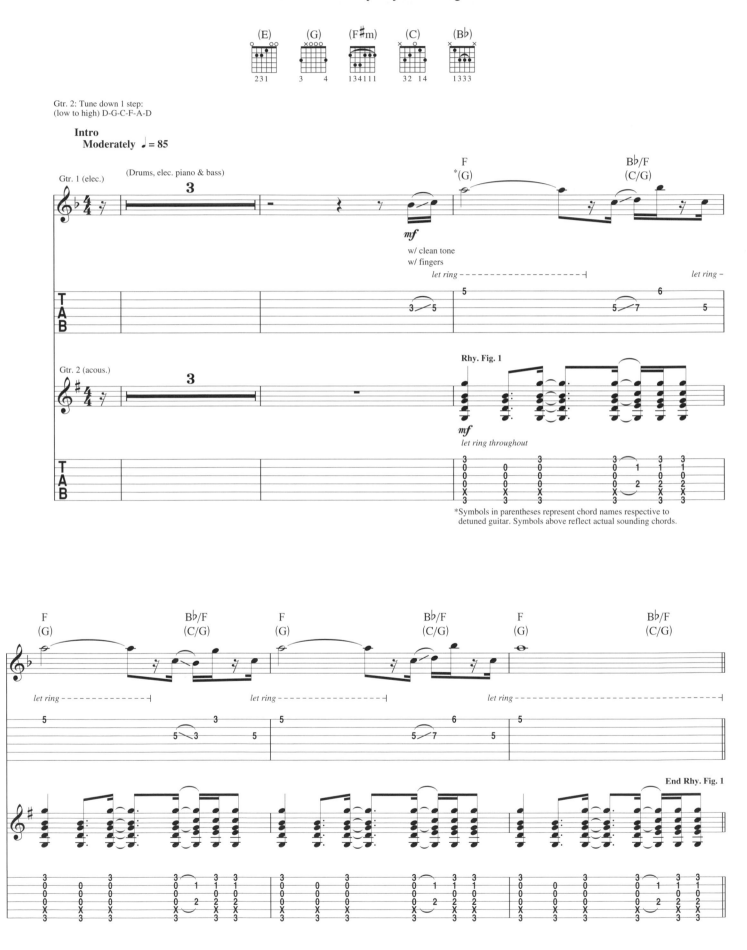

Verse

Gtr. 1 tacet
Gtr. 2: w/ Rhy. Fig. 1

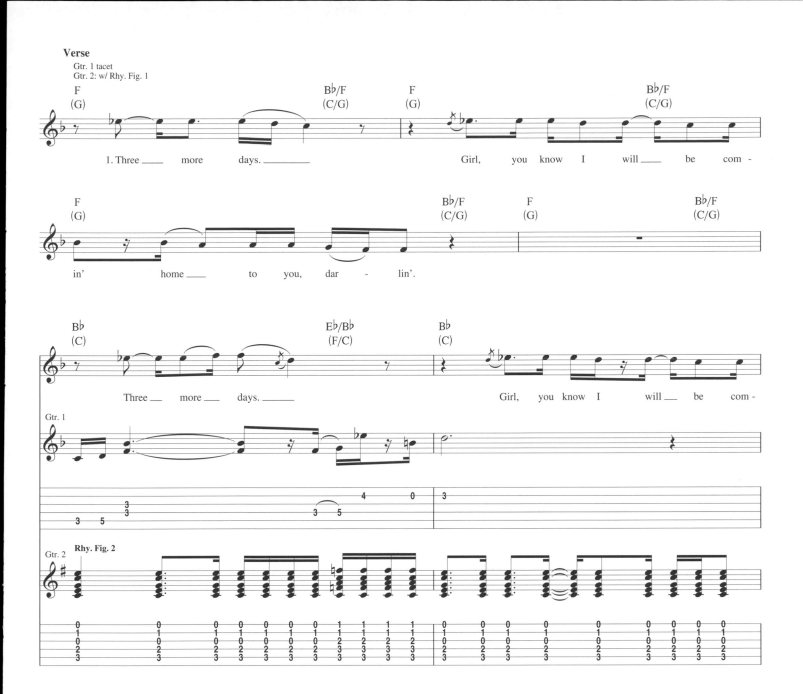

1. Three ____ more ____ days. _____ Girl, you know I will ____ be com-

in' ____ home ____ to you, dar - lin'.

Three ____ more ____ days. _____ Girl, you know I will ____ be com-

in' ____ home _____ to you, dar - lin'.

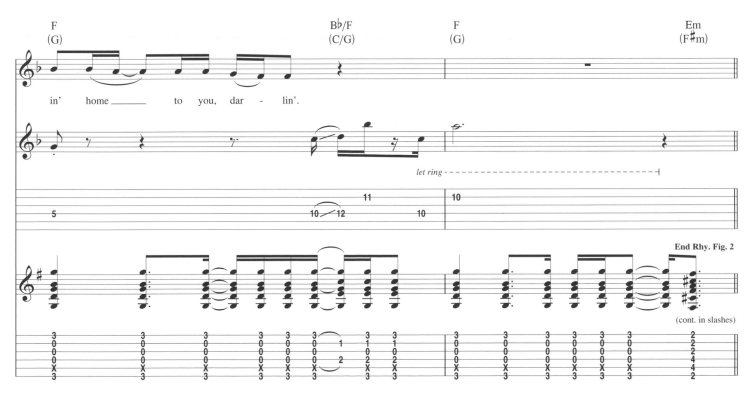

21

Pre-Chorus

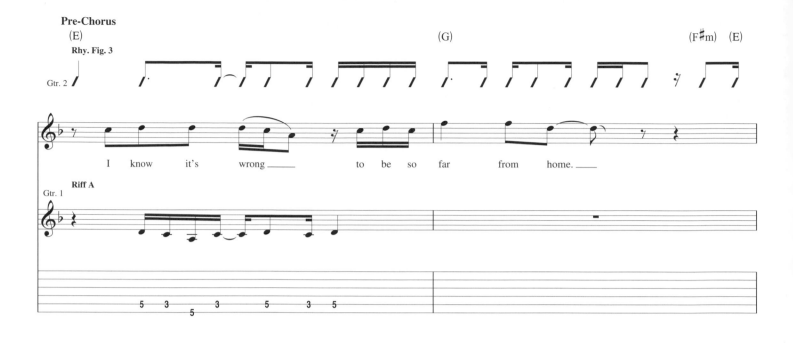

I know it's wrong _____ to be so far from home. _____

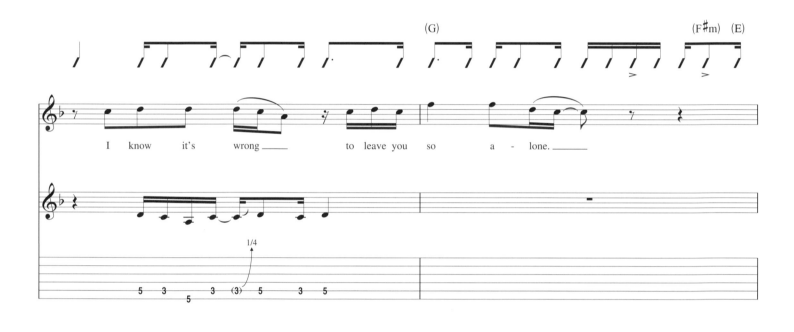

I know it's wrong _____ to leave you so a - lone. _____

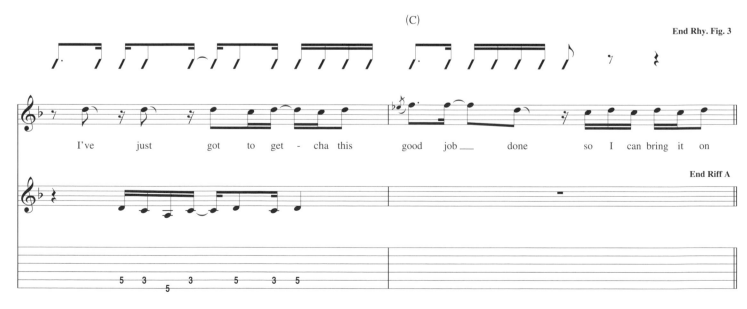

I've just got to get - cha this good job _____ done so I can bring it on

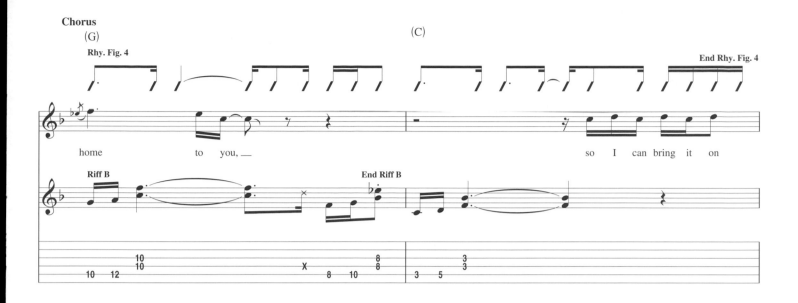

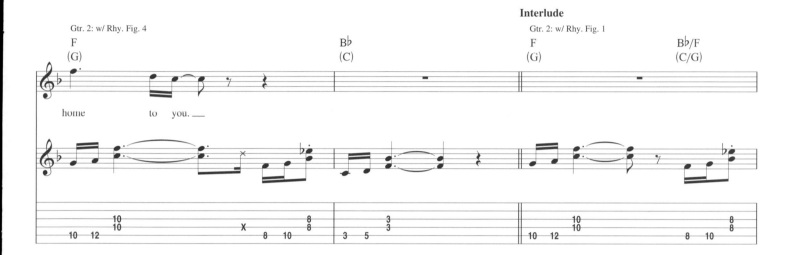

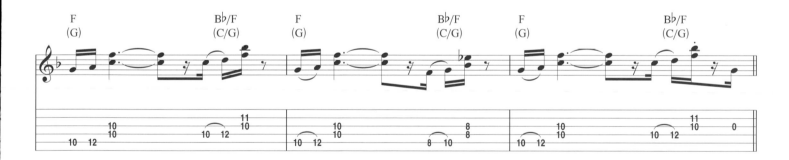

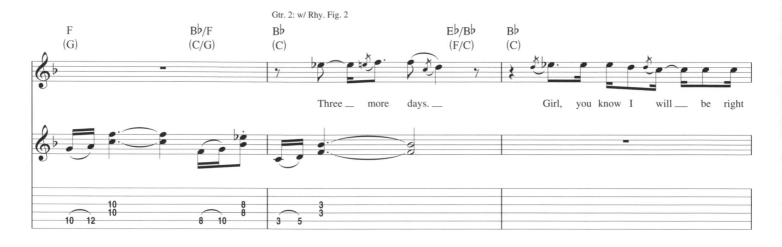

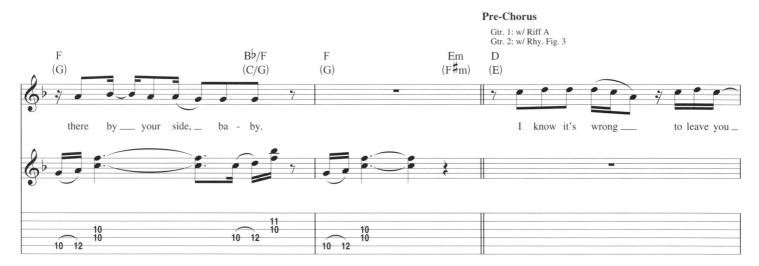

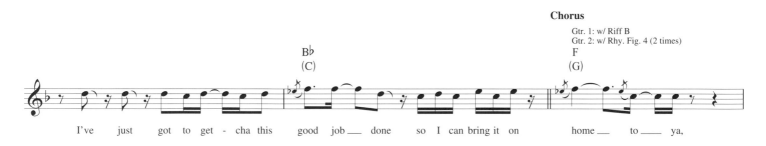

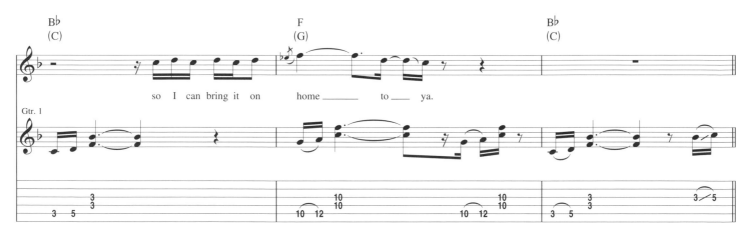

Interlude

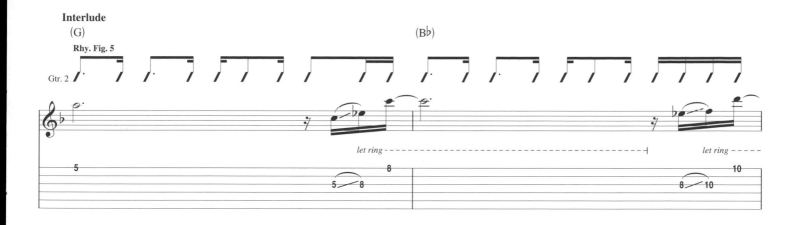

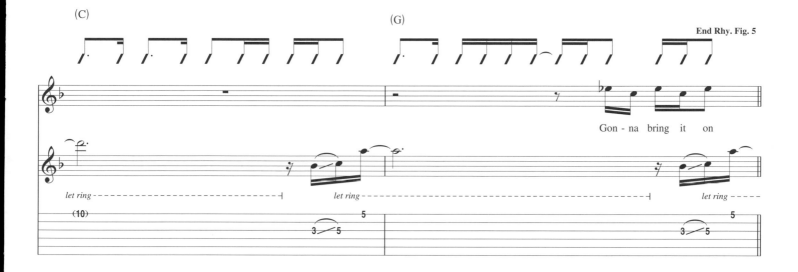

Gon - na bring it on

Bridge

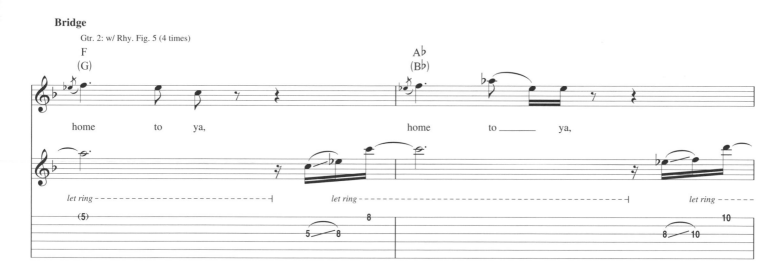

home   to   ya,   home   to _____ ya,

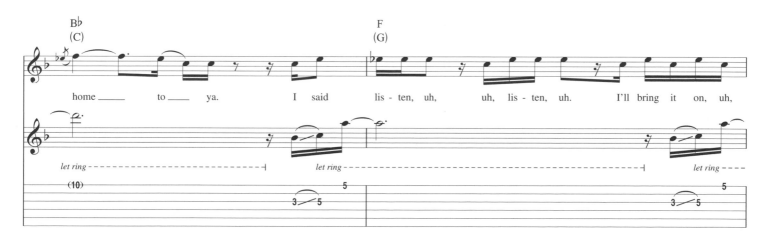

home _____ to _____ ya.   I said   lis - ten, uh,   uh, lis - ten, uh.   I'll bring it on, uh,

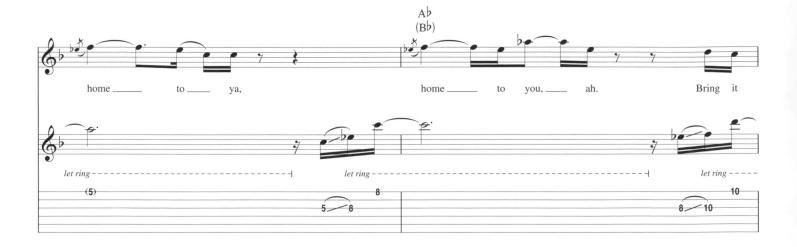

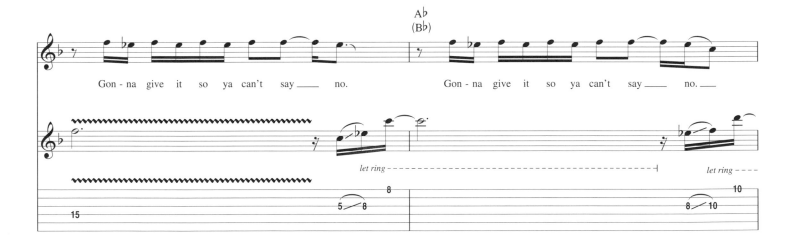

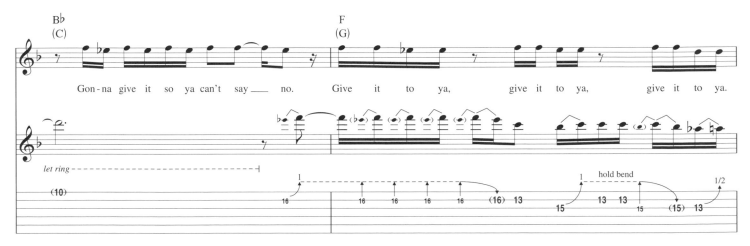

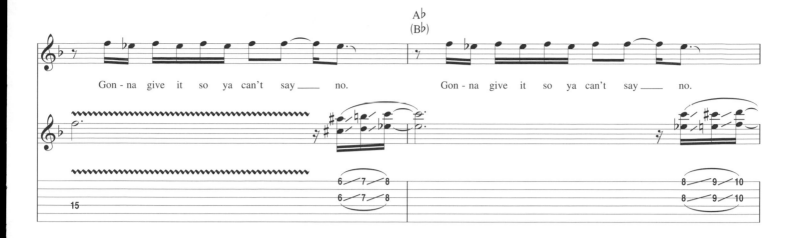

Gon - na give it so ya can't say ___ no.   Gon - na give it so ya can't say ___ no.

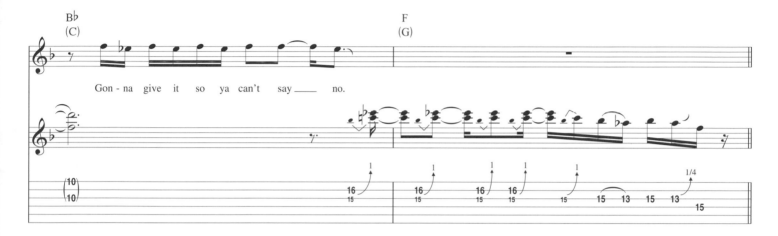

Gon - na give it so ya can't say ___ no.

Outro

Gtr. 2: w/ Rhy. Fig. 4 (till fade)

Begin fade

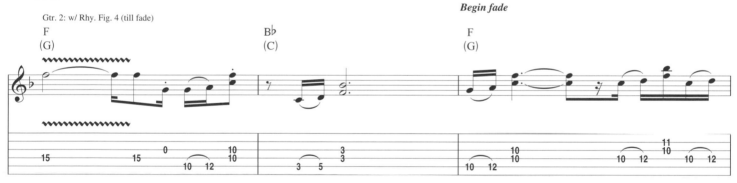

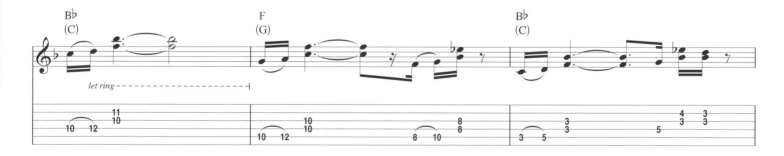

Fade out

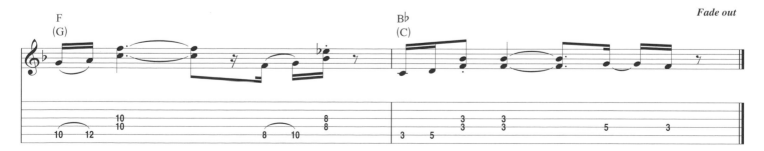

Can I Stay

Words and Music by Ray LaMontagne

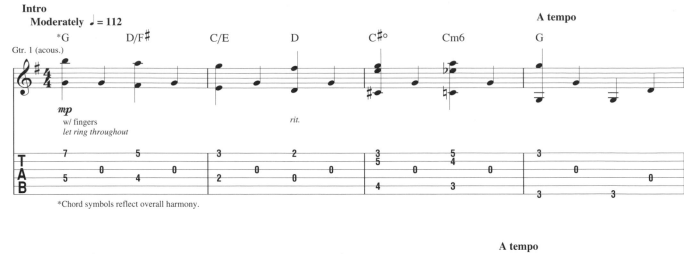

*Chord symbols reflect overall harmony.

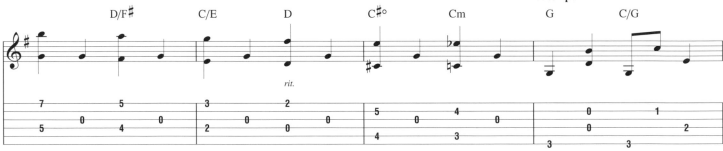

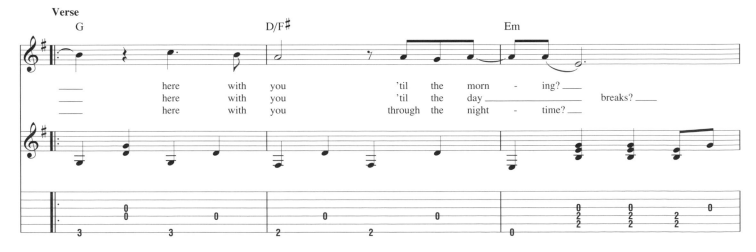

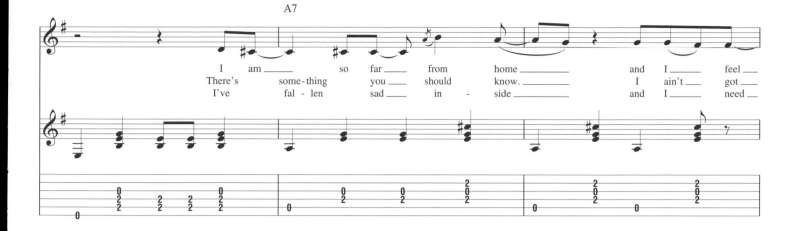

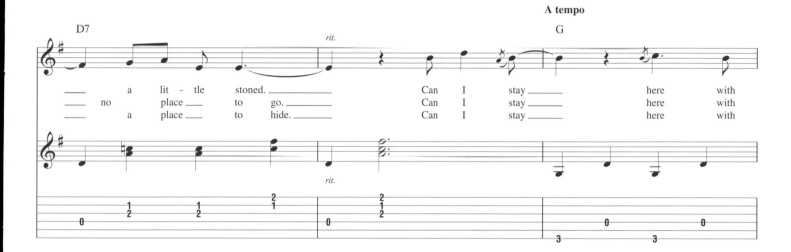

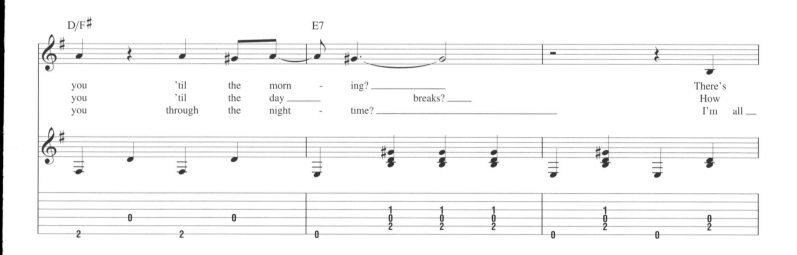

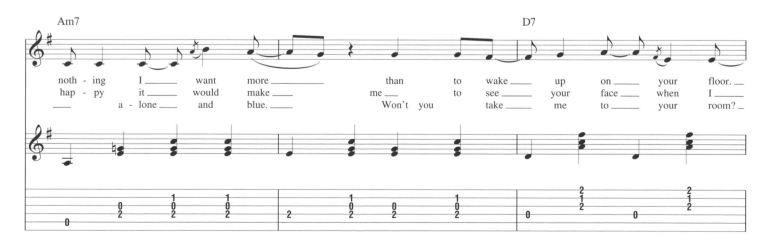

Chorus

Lay with me ____ in your thin - nest dress. ____

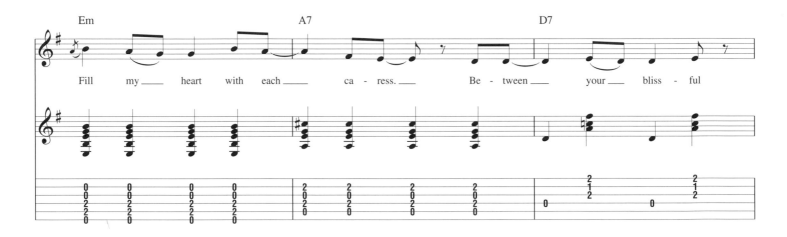

Fill my ____ heart with each ____ ca - ress. ____ Be - tween ____ your ____ bliss - ful

kiss - es, ____ whis - per, "Dar - ling, is ____ this love?"

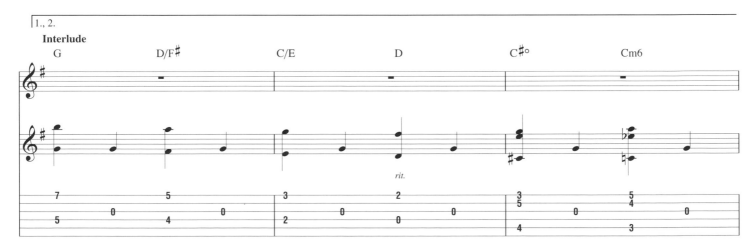

1., 2.

Interlude

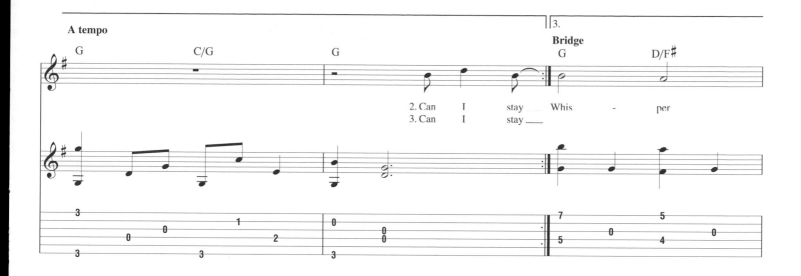

2. Can I stay Whis - per
3. Can I stay ___

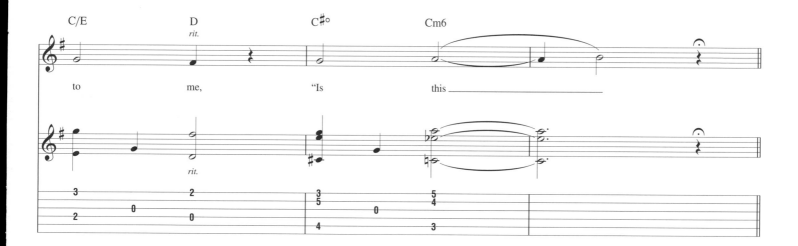

to me, "Is this ___

Outro

love?" ___

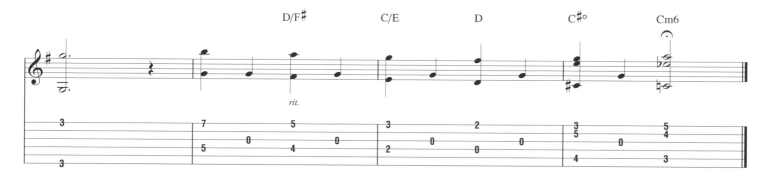

You Can Bring Me Flowers

Words and Music by Ray LaMontagne

Gtr. 1: Capo III

Gtr. 2: Open G tuning:
(low to high) D-G-D-G-B-D

*Symbols in parentheses represent chord names respective to capoed guitar.
Symbols above reflect actual sounding chords. Capoed fret is "0" in tab.
Chord symbols reflect implied harmony.

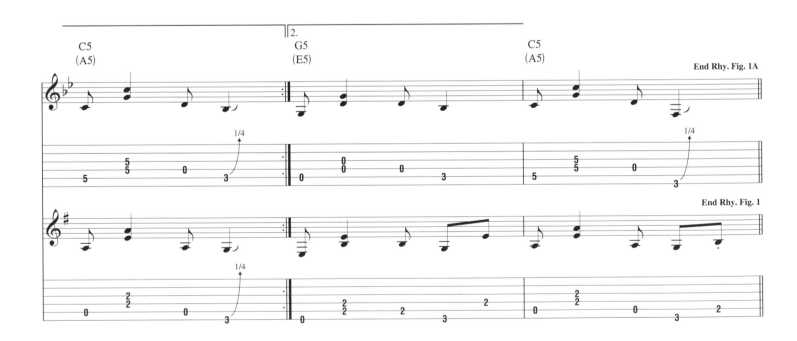

Gtrs. 1 & 2: w/ Rhy. Figs. 1 & 1A

Sing this sad, _____ sad _____ song.
and sing this this sad, _____ sad, _____ song.

Gtrs. 1 & 2: w/ Rhy. Figs. 1 & 1A
G5 (E5)   C5 (A5)   G5 (E5)   C5 (A5)

You ___ can ___ bring ___ me flow - ers, ba - by,

To Coda ⊕

G5 (E5)   C5 (A5)   G5 (E5)   C5 (A5)

when I'm ___ dead and gone. ___

1.
Interlude
Gtrs. 1 & 2: w/ Rhy. Figs. 1 & 1A (last 4 meas.)
G5 (E5)   C5 (A5)   G5 (E5)   C5 (A5)

G5 (E5)   C5 (A5)   G5 (E5)   N.C.

Gtr. 2   **Rhy. Fig. 2**   **End Rhy. Fig. 2**

Gtr. 1

Gtrs. 1 & 2: w/ Rhy. Figs. 1 & 1A

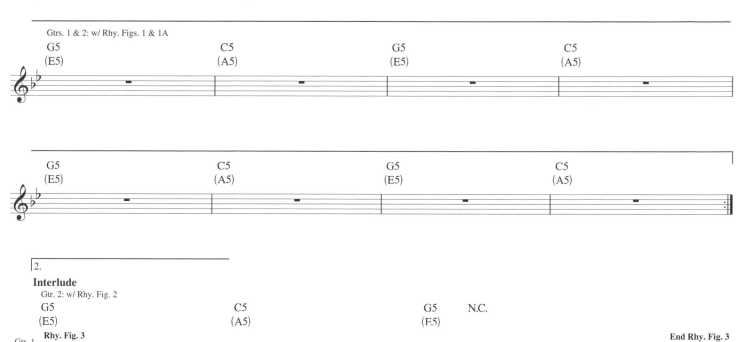

2.

Interlude

Gtr. 2: w/ Rhy. Fig. 2

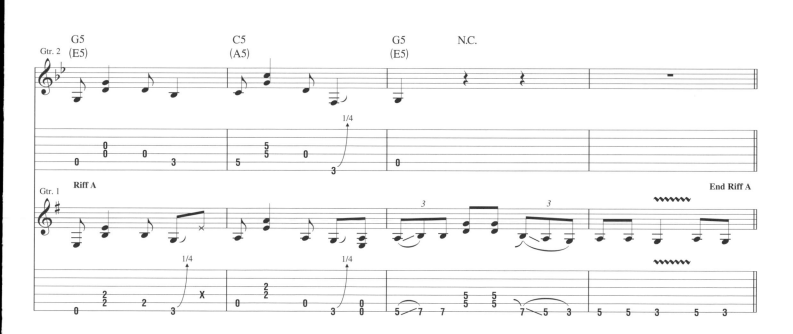

2nd time, D.S. al Coda

Gtrs. 1 & 2: w/ Rhy. Figs. 1 & 1A (1st 4 meas., 2 times)

⊕ Coda

Interlude

Gtr. 1: w/ Rhy. Fig. 3 (2 times)
Gtr. 2: w/ Rhy. Fig. 2 (2 times)

Gone Away From Me

Words and Music by Ray LaMontagne

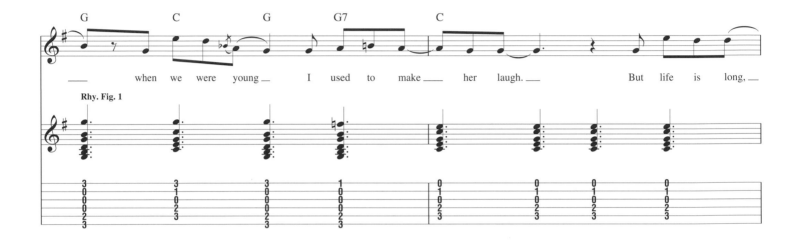

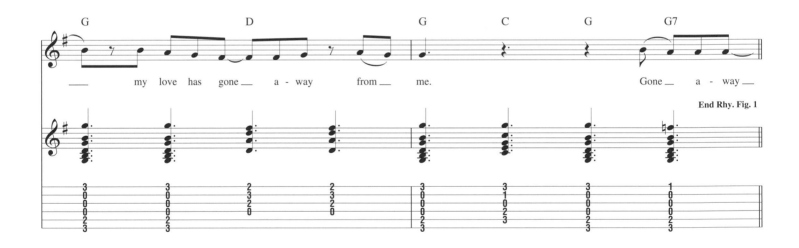

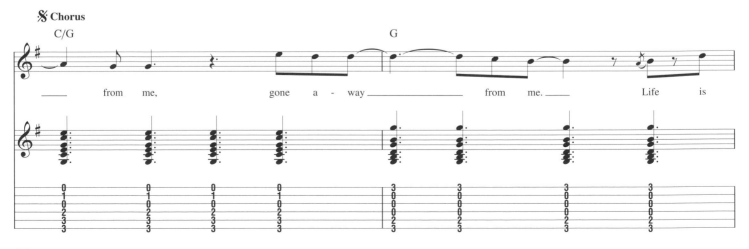

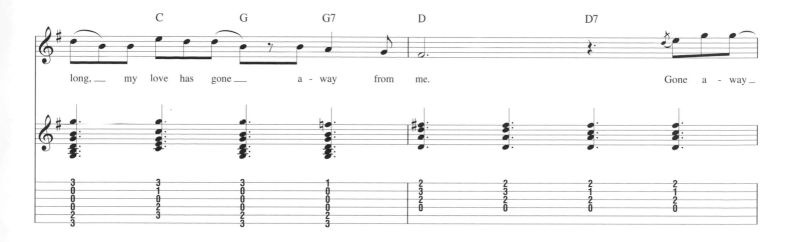

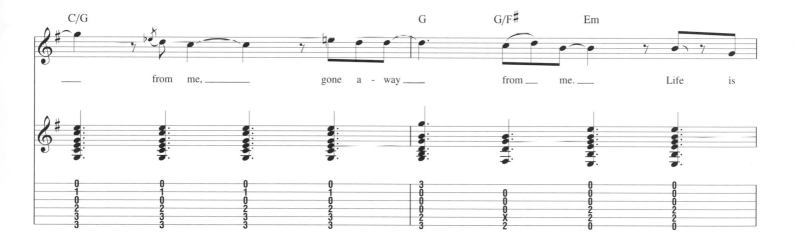

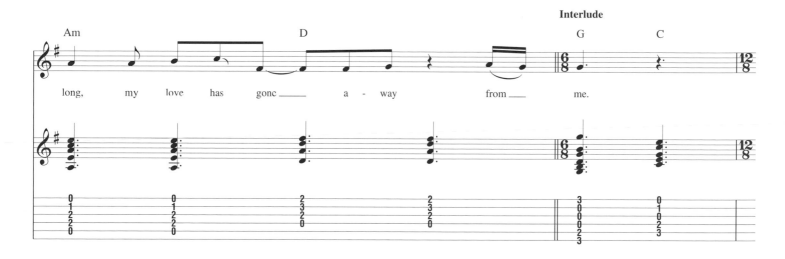

To Coda 1
To Coda 2

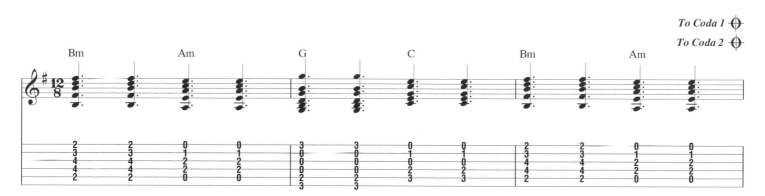

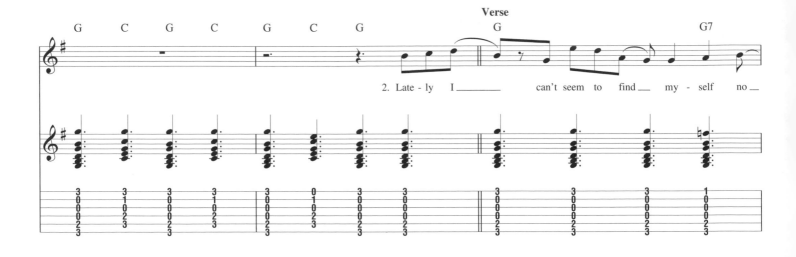

2. Late - ly I _____ can't seem to find ____ my - self no ____

____ sleep at all. ____ Late - ly I _____ just lie a - wake ____ in here ____ and dream ____ of the time ____

Gtr. 1: w/ Rhy. Fig. 1

____ when she was mine, _____ felt like I had ____ it all. _____ But life is long, ____

D.S. al Coda 1

____ my love has gone ____ a - way from ____ me. Gone ____ a - way ____

Coda 1

Bridge

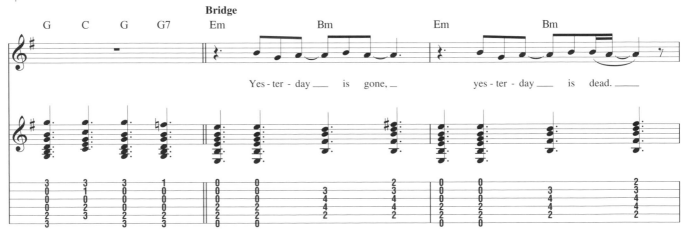

Yes - ter - day ____ is gone, ____ yes - ter - day ____ is dead. ____

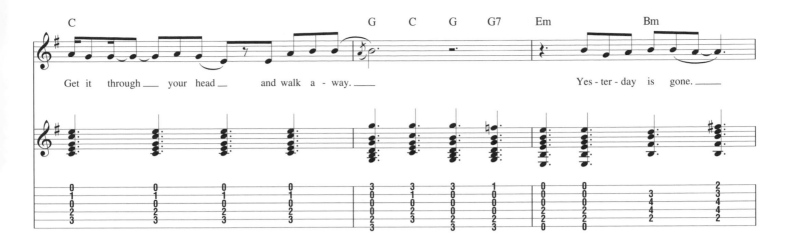

Get it through your head and walk a - way. Yes - ter - day is gone.

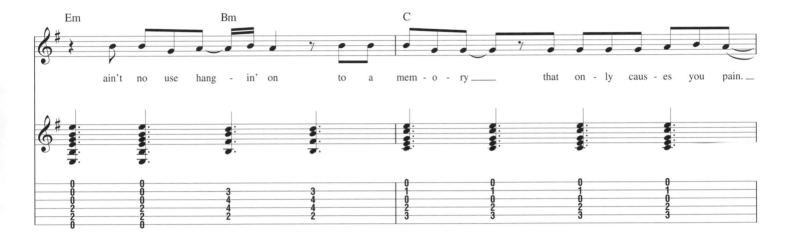

ain't no use hang - in' on to a mem - o - ry that on - ly caus - es you pain.

D.S.S. al Coda 2

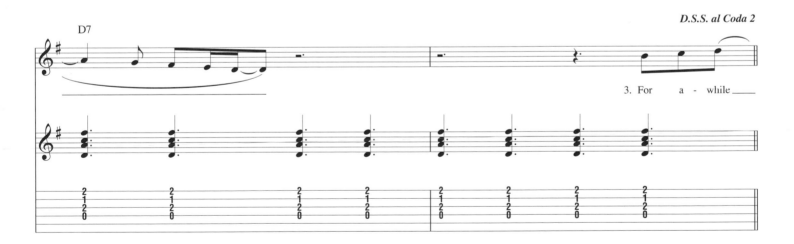

3. For a - while

Coda 2

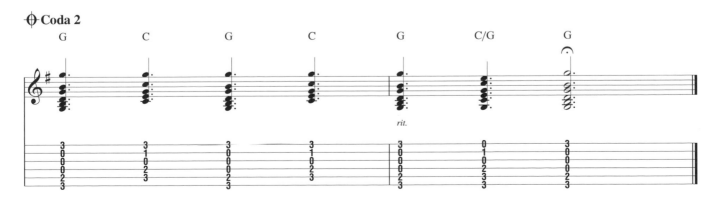

Lesson Learned

Words and Music by Ray LaMontagne

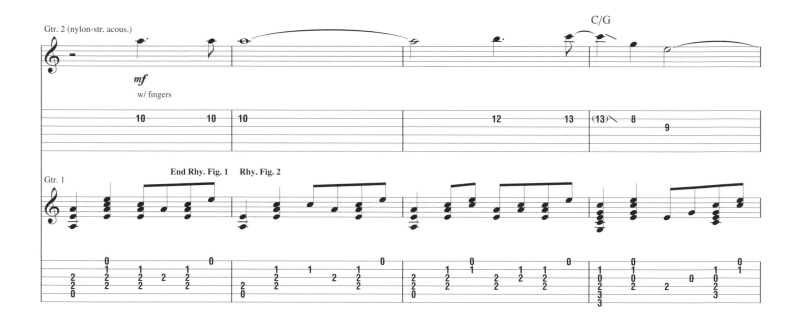

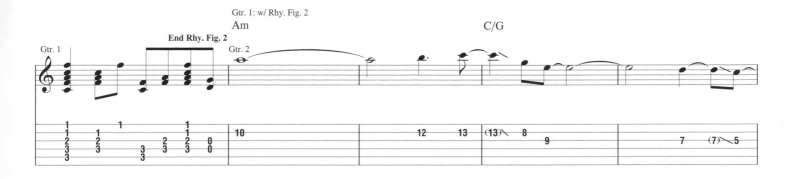

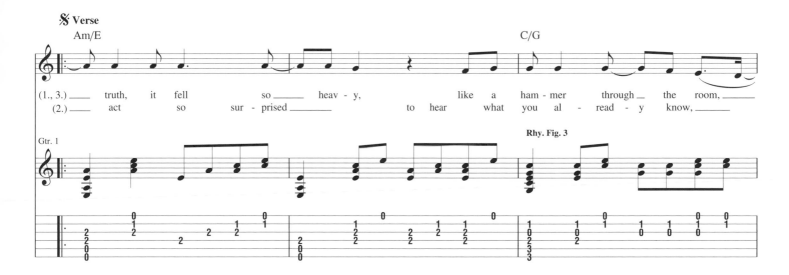

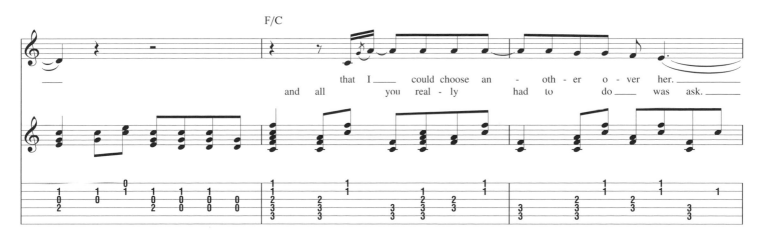

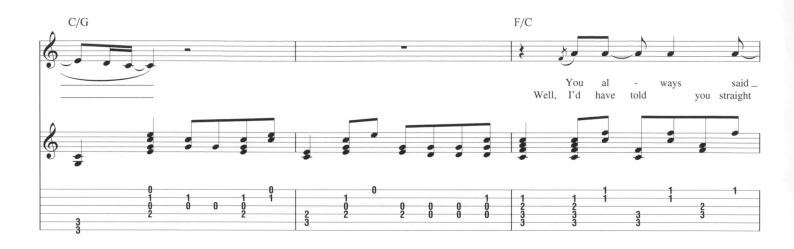

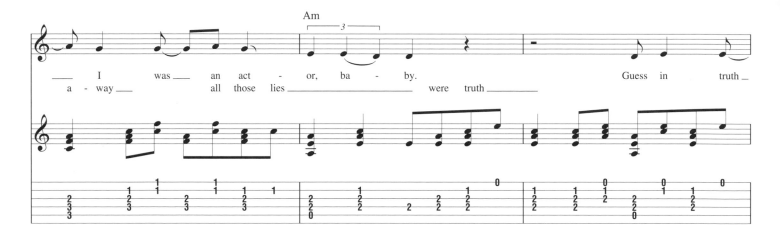

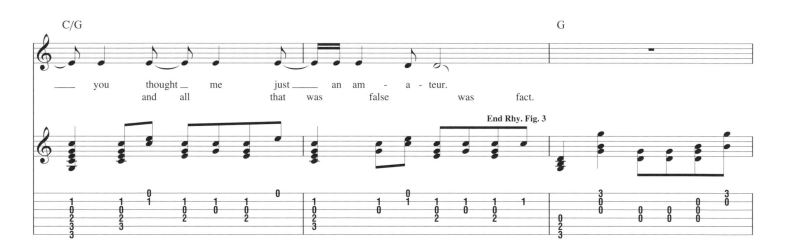

Gtr. 1: w/ Rhy. Fig. 2 (last 2 meas.)   Gtr. 1: w/ Rhy. Fig. 1
Am/E

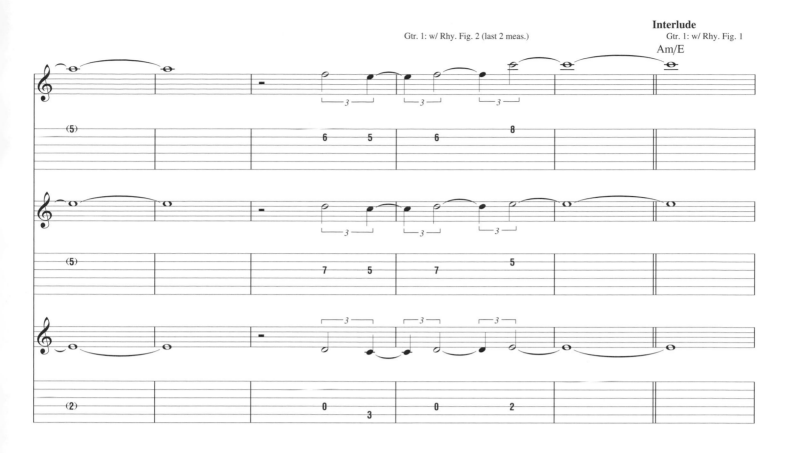

Gtrs. 2, 3 & 4 tacet   *D.S. al Coda*

3. Well, the _____

Coda
C/G   F

Shall we   call _____ this   a   les - son _____ learned? _____

Outro
Am/E
                                                     rit.

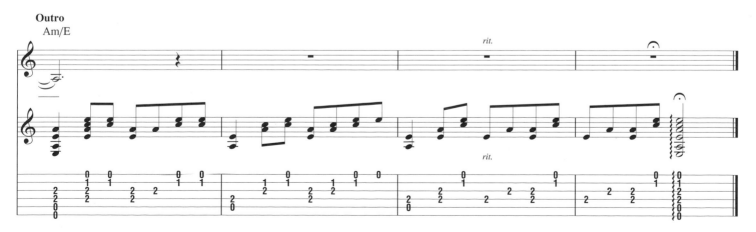

rit.

Truly, Madly, Deeply

Words and Music by Ray LaMontagne

Tune down 1/2 step:
(low to high) E♭-A♭-D♭-G♭-B♭-E♭

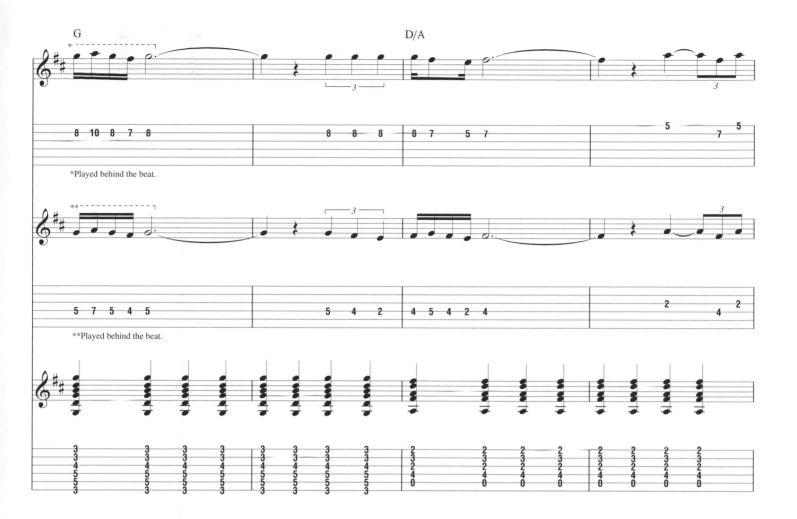

*Played behind the beat.

**Played behind the beat.

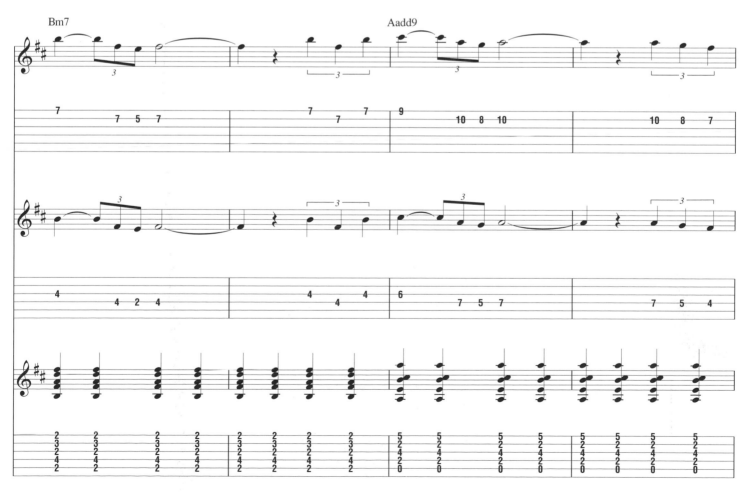

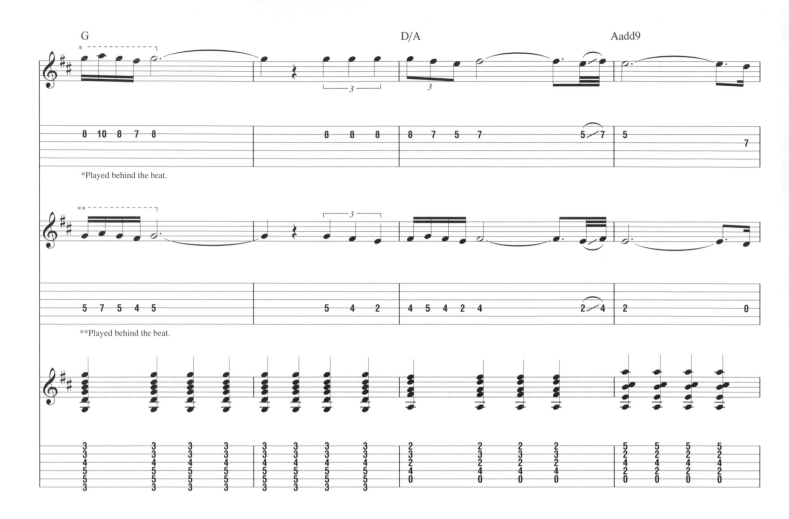

*Played behind the beat.

**Played behind the beat.

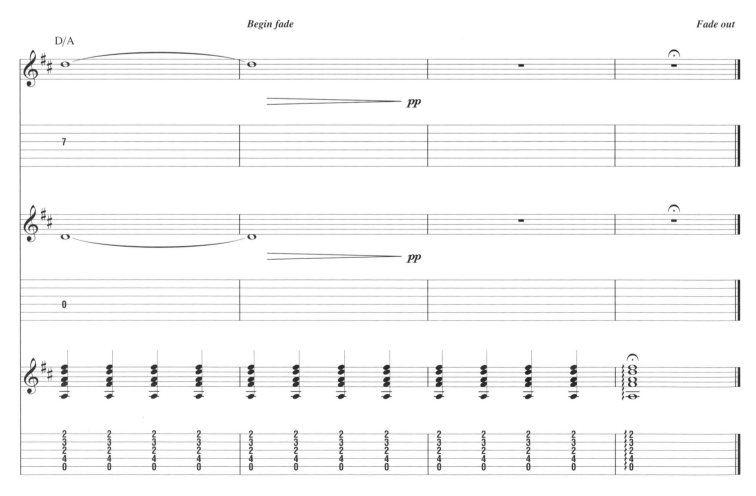

Till the Sun Turns Black

Words and Music by Ray LaMontagne

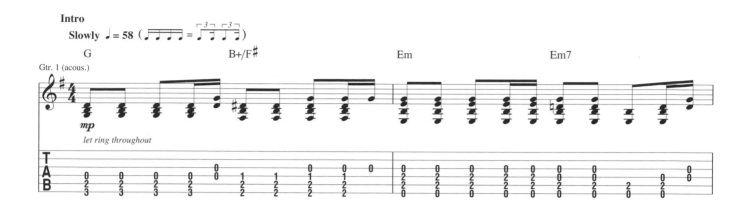

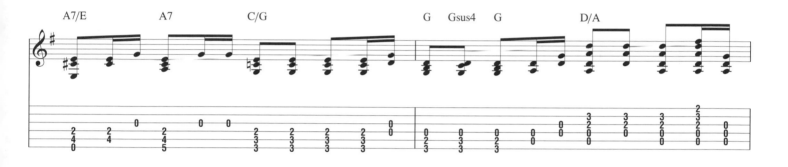

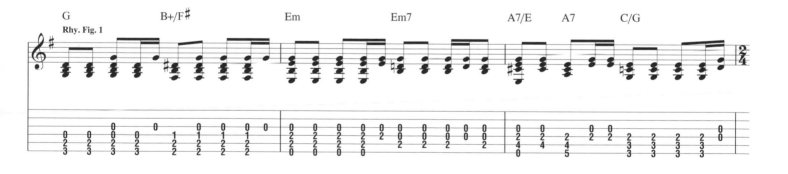

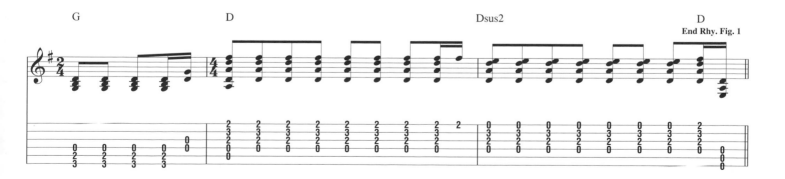

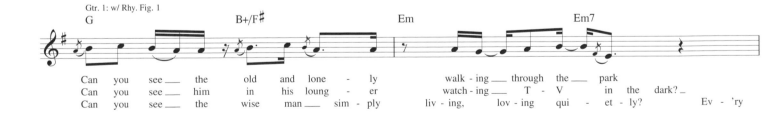
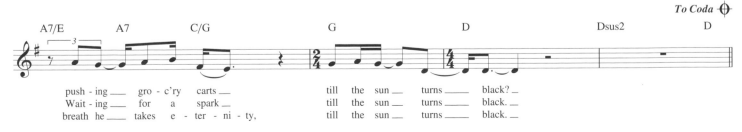

Interlude

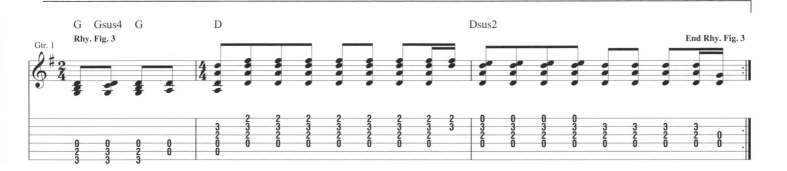

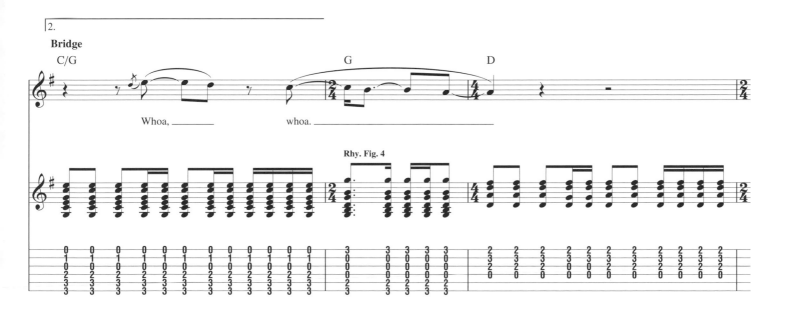

Bridge

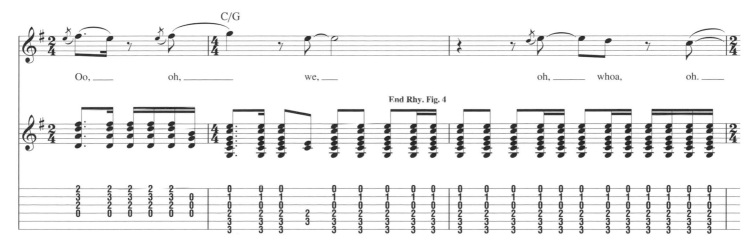

Oo, _____ oh, _____ we, _____ who are _____

Interlude

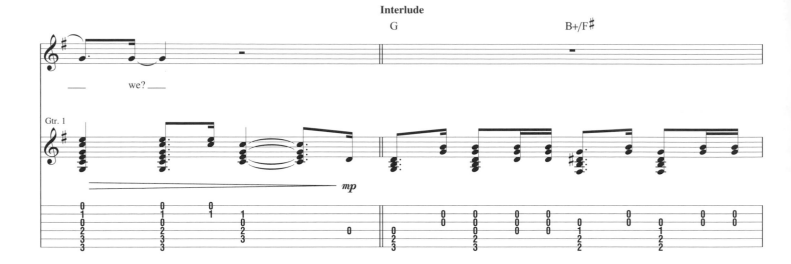

_____ we? _____

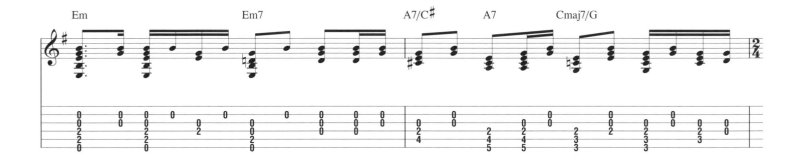

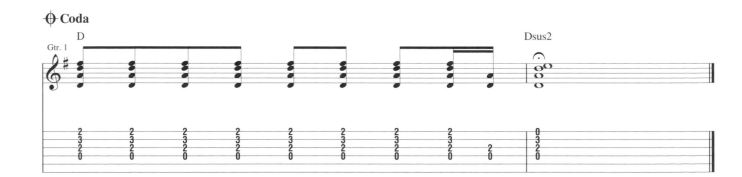

Within You

Words and Music by Ray LaMontagne

Gtr. 1: Capo II

Gtr. 2: Open D tuning:
(low to high) D-A-D-F♯-A-D

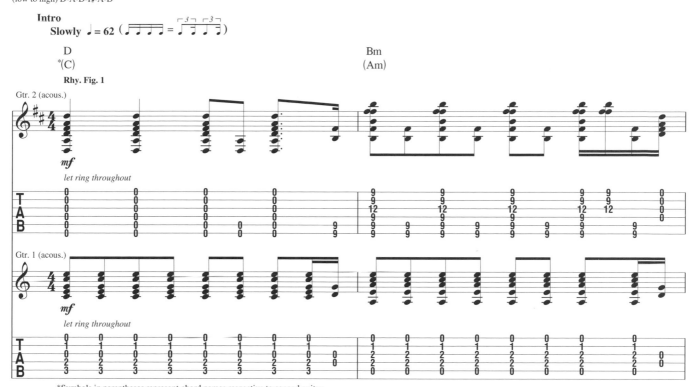

*Symbols in parentheses represent chord names respective to capoed guitar.
Symbols above reflect actual sounding chords. Capoed fret is "0" in tab.

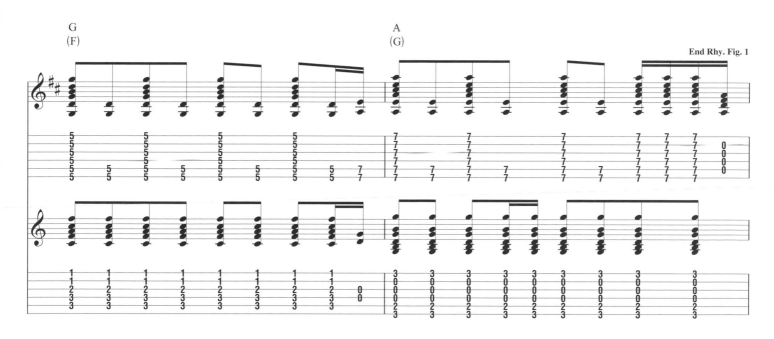

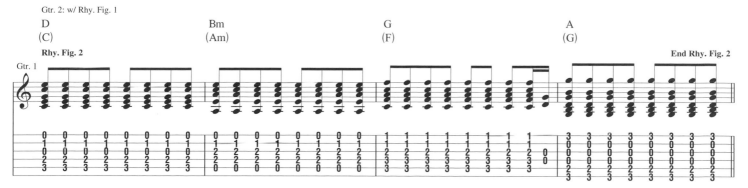

Verse

Gtr. 1: w/ Rhy. Fig. 2 (2 times)
Gtr. 2: w/ Rhy. Fig. 1 (2 times)

D
(C)
Bm
(Am)
G
(F)
A
(G)

1. War _____ is not the an - swer. _____ The an - swer _____ is with-in _____ you.

D
(C)
Bm
(Am)
G
(F)
A
(G)

War _____ is not the an - swer. _____ The an - swer _____ is with-in _____ you.

Chorus

Gtr. 1: w/ Rhy. Fig. 2 (2 times)
Gtr. 2: w/ Rhy. Fig. 1 (2 times)

D
(C)
Bm
(Am)
G
(F)
A
(G)

Voc. Fig. 1

End Voc. Fig. 1

Love, _____ love. _____

D
(C)
Bm
(Am)
G
(F)
A
(G)

Love, _____ love. _____

Interlude

Gtr. 1: w/ Rhy. Fig. 2
Gtr. 2: w/ Rhy. Fig. 1

D
(C)
Bm
(Am)
G
(F)
A
(G)

Verse

Bkgd. Voc.: w/ Voc. Fig. 1
Gtr. 1: w/ Rhy. Fig. 2
Gtr. 2: w/ Rhy. Fig. 1

D
(C)
Bm
(Am)
G
(F)
A
(G)

2. War _____ is not the an - swer. _____ The an - swer _____ is with-in _____ you.

Chorus

Bkgd. Voc.: w/ Voc. Fig. 1
Gtr. 1: w/ Rhy. Fig. 2 (7 1/2 times)
Gtr. 2: w/ Rhy. Fig. 1 (6 times)

D
(C)
Bm
(Am)
G
(F)
A
(G)

Love, _____ love. _____

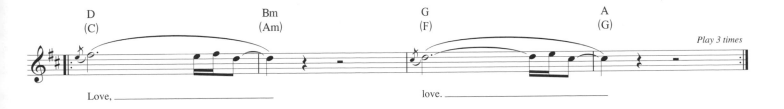

Love, _____ love. _____

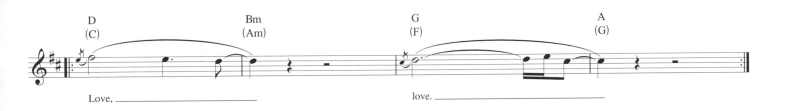

Love, _____ love. _____

Gtr. 2 tacet

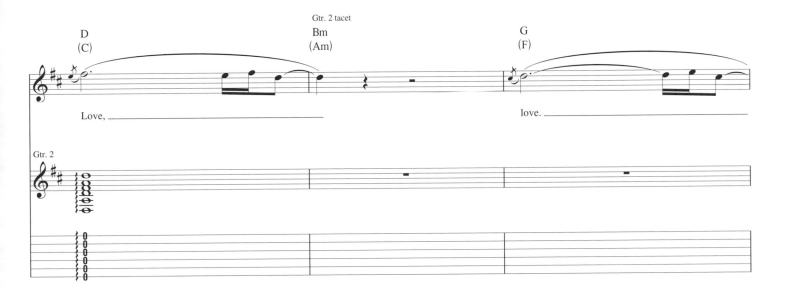

Love, _____ love. _____

Gtr. 2

_____ Love, _____

Interlude

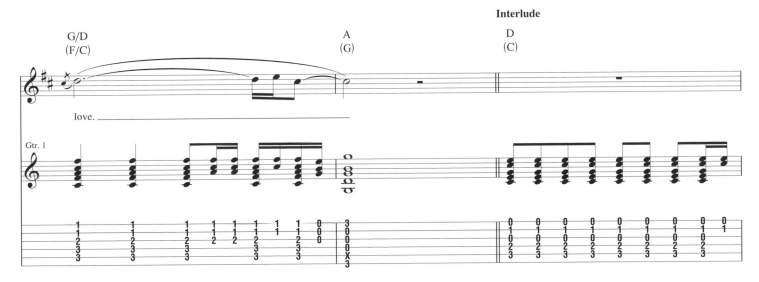

love. _____

Gtr. 1

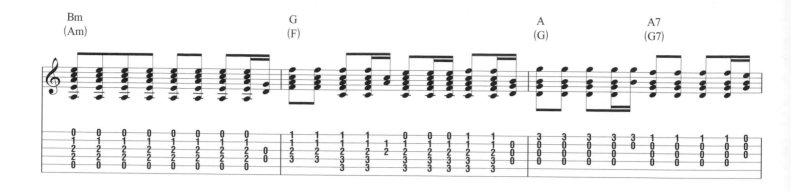

Gtr. 1: w/ Rhy. Fig. 2 (2 times)
Gtr. 2: w/ Rhy. Fig. 1 (2 times)

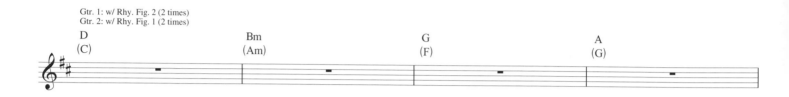

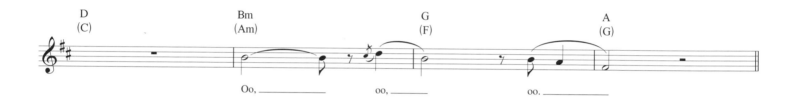

Oo, _____ oo, _____ oo. _____

Outro-Chorus

Gtr. 1: w/ Rhy. Fig. 2 (till fade)
Gtr. 2: w/ Rhy. Fig. 1 (till fade)

*__Begin fade__

Love, _____ love, _____

*Except strings & brass.

Love, _____ love. _____

**__Fade out__

rit.

**As before

58

Guitar Notation Legend

Guitar music can be notated three different ways: on a *musical staff*, in *tablature*, and in *rhythm slashes*.

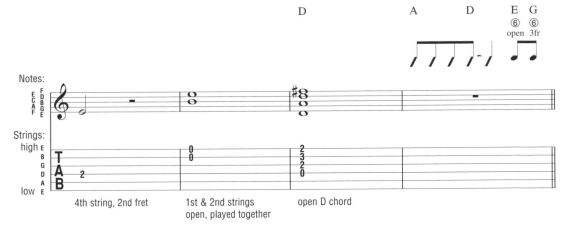

RHYTHM SLASHES are written above the staff. Strum chords in the rhythm indicated. Use the chord diagrams found at the top of the first page of the transcription for the appropriate chord voicings. Round noteheads indicate single notes.

THE MUSICAL STAFF shows pitches and rhythms and is divided by bar lines into measures. Pitches are named after the first seven letters of the alphabet.

TABLATURE graphically represents the guitar fingerboard. Each horizontal line represents a string, and each number represents a fret.

Definitions for Special Guitar Notation

HALF-STEP BEND: Strike the note and bend up 1/2 step.

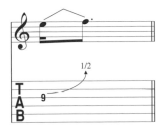

WHOLE-STEP BEND: Strike the note and bend up one step.

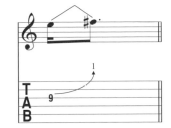

GRACE NOTE BEND: Strike the note and immediately bend up as indicated.

SLIGHT (MICROTONE) BEND: Strike the note and bend up 1/4 step.

BEND AND RELEASE: Strike the note and bend up as indicated, then release back to the original note. Only the first note is struck.

PRE-BEND: Bend the note as indicated, then strike it.

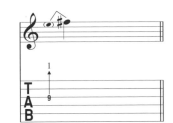

PRE-BEND AND RELEASE: Bend the note as indicated. Strike it and release the bend back to the original note.

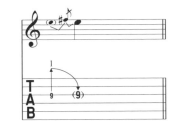

UNISON BEND: Strike the two notes simultaneously and bend the lower note up to the pitch of the higher.

VIBRATO: The string is vibrated by rapidly bending and releasing the note with the fretting hand.

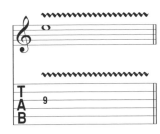

WIDE VIBRATO: The pitch is varied to a greater degree by vibrating with the fretting hand.

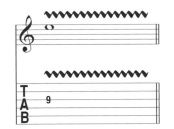

HAMMER-ON: Strike the first (lower) note with one finger, then sound the higher note (on the same string) with another finger by fretting it without picking.

PULL-OFF: Place both fingers on the notes to be sounded. Strike the first note and without picking, pull the finger off to sound the second (lower) note.

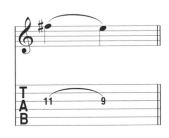

LEGATO SLIDE: Strike the first note and then slide the same fret-hand finger up or down to the second note. The second note is not struck.

SHIFT SLIDE: Same as legato slide, except the second note is struck.

TRILL: Very rapidly alternate between the notes indicated by continuously hammering on and pulling off.

TAPPING: Hammer ("tap") the fret indicated with the pick-hand index or middle finger and pull off to the note fretted by the fret hand.

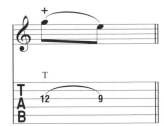

NATURAL HARMONIC: Strike the note while the fret-hand lightly touches the string directly over the fret indicated.

PINCH HARMONIC: The note is fretted normally and a harmonic is produced by adding the edge of the thumb or the tip of the index finger of the pick hand to the normal pick attack.

HARP HARMONIC: The note is fretted normally and a harmonic is produced by gently resting the pick hand's index finger directly above the indicated fret (in parentheses) while the pick hand's thumb or pick assists by plucking the appropriate string.

PICK SCRAPE: The edge of the pick is rubbed down (or up) the string, producing a scratchy sound.

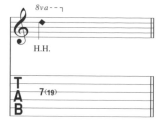

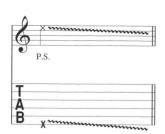

MUFFLED STRINGS: A percussive sound is produced by laying the fret hand across the string(s) without depressing, and striking them with the pick hand.

PALM MUTING: The note is partially muted by the pick hand lightly touching the string(s) just before the bridge.

RAKE: Drag the pick across the strings indicated with a single motion.

TREMOLO PICKING: The note is picked as rapidly and continuously as possible.

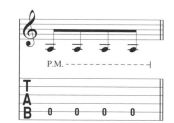

ARPEGGIATE: Play the notes of the chord indicated by quickly rolling them from bottom to top.

VIBRATO BAR DIVE AND RETURN: The pitch of the note or chord is dropped a specified number of steps (in rhythm), then returned to the original pitch.

VIBRATO BAR SCOOP: Depress the bar just before striking the note, then quickly release the bar.

VIBRATO BAR DIP: Strike the note and then immediately drop a specified number of steps, then release back to the original pitch.

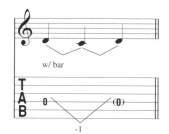

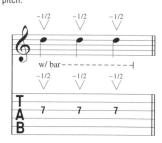

Additional Musical Definitions

(accent) • Accentuate note (play it louder).

(accent) • Accentuate note with great intensity.

(staccato) • Play the note short.

• Downstroke

V • Upstroke

D.S. al Coda • Go back to the sign (𝄋), then play until the measure marked *"To Coda,"* then skip to the section labelled "**Coda**."

D.C. al Fine • Go back to the beginning of the song and play until the measure marked *"**Fine**"* (end).

Rhy. Fig. • Label used to recall a recurring accompaniment pattern (usually chordal).

Riff • Label used to recall composed, melodic lines (usually single notes) which recur.

Fill • Label used to identify a brief melodic figure which is to be inserted into the arrangement.

Rhy. Fill • A chordal version of a Fill.

tacet • Instrument is silent (drops out).

• Repeat measures between signs.

• When a repeated section has different endings, play the first ending only the first time and the second ending only the second time.

NOTE: Tablature numbers in parentheses mean:
1. The note is being sustained over a system (note in standard notation is tied), or
2. The note is sustained, but a new articulation (such as a hammer-on, pull-off, slide or vibrato) begins, or
3. The note is a barely audible "ghost" note (note in standard notation is also in parentheses).

GUITAR *signature licks*

Signature Licks book/CD packs provide a step-by-step breakdown of "right from the record" riffs, licks, and solos so you can jam along with your favorite bands. They contain performance notes and an overview of each artist's or group's style, with note-for-note transcriptions in notes and tab. The CDs feature full-band demos at both normal and slow speeds.

BEST OF ACOUSTIC GUITAR
00695640 ....$19.95

AEROSMITH 1973-1979
00695106 ....$22.95

AEROSMITH 1979-1998
00695219 ....$22.95

BEST OF AGGRO-METAL
00695592 ....$19.95

BEST OF CHET ATKINS
00695752 ....$22.95

THE BEACH BOYS DEFINITIVE COLLECTION
00695683 ....$22.95

BEST OF THE BEATLES FOR ACOUSTIC GUITAR
00695453 ....$22.95

THE BEATLES BASS
00695283 ....$22.95

THE BEATLES FAVORITES
00695096 ....$24.95

THE BEATLES HITS
00695049 ....$24.95

BEST OF GEORGE BENSON
00695418 ....$22.95

BEST OF BLACK SABBATH
00695249 ....$22.95

BEST OF BLINK - 182
00695704 ....$22.95

BEST OF BLUES GUITAR
00695846 ....$19.95

BLUES GUITAR CLASSICS
00695177 ....$19.95

BLUES/ROCK GUITAR MASTERS
00695348 ....$19.95

BEST OF CHARLIE CHRISTIAN
00695584 ....$22.95

BEST OF ERIC CLAPTON
00695038 ....$24.95

ERIC CLAPTON – THE BLUESMAN
00695040 ....$22.95

ERIC CLAPTON – FROM THE ALBUM UNPLUGGED
00695250 ....$24.95

BEST OF CREAM
00695251 ....$22.95

DEEP PURPLE – GREATEST HITS
00695625 ....$22.95

THE BEST OF DEF LEPPARD
00696516 ....$22.95

THE DOORS
00695373 ....$22.95

FAMOUS ROCK GUITAR SOLOS
00695590 ....$19.95

BEST OF FOO FIGHTERS
00695481 ....$22.95

GREATEST GUITAR SOLOS OF ALL TIME
00695301 ....$19.95

BEST OF GRANT GREEN
00695747 ....$22.95

GUITAR INSTRUMENTAL HITS
00695309 ....$19.95

GUITAR RIFFS OF THE '60S
00695218 ....$19.95

BEST OF GUNS N' ROSES
00695183 ....$22.95

HARD ROCK SOLOS
00695591 ....$19.95

JIMI HENDRIX
00696560 ....$24.95

HOT COUNTRY GUITAR
00695580 ....$19.95

BEST OF JAZZ GUITAR
00695586 ....$24.95

ERIC JOHNSON
00699317 ....$22.95

ROBERT JOHNSON
00695264 ....$22.95

THE ESSENTIAL ALBERT KING
00695713 ....$22.95

B.B. KING – THE DEFINITIVE COLLECTION
00695635 ....$22.95

THE KINKS
00695553 ....$22.95

BEST OF KISS
00699413 ....$22.95

MARK KNOPFLER
00695178 ....$22.95

BEST OF YNGWIE MALMSTEEN
00695669 ....$22.95

BEST OF PAT MARTINO
00695632 ....$22.95

MEGADETH
00695041 ....$22.95

WES MONTGOMERY
00695387 ....$22.95

BEST OF NIRVANA
00695483 ....$24.95

THE OFFSPRING
00695852 ....$24.95

VERY BEST OF OZZY OSBOURNE
00695431 ....$22.95

BEST OF JOE PASS
00695730 ....$22.95

PINK FLOYD – EARLY CLASSICS
00695566 ....$22.95

THE POLICE
00695724 ....$22.95

THE GUITARS OF ELVIS
00696507 ....$22.95

BEST OF QUEEN
00695097 ....$22.95

BEST OF RAGE AGAINST THE MACHINE
00695480 ....$22.95

RED HOT CHILI PEPPERS
00695173 ....$22.95

RED HOT CHILI PEPPERS – GREATEST HITS
00695828 ....$24.95

BEST OF DJANGO REINHARDT
00695660 ....$22.95

BEST OF ROCK
00695884 ....$19.95

BEST OF ROCK 'N' ROLL GUITAR
00695559 ....$19.95

BEST OF ROCKABILLY GUITAR
00695785 ....$19.95

THE ROLLING STONES
00695079 ....$22.95

BEST OF JOE SATRIANI
00695216 ....$22.95

BEST OF SILVERCHAIR
00695488 ....$22.95

THE BEST OF SOUL GUITAR
00695703 ....$19.95

BEST OF SOUTHERN ROCK
00695703 ....$19.95

ROD STEWART
00695663 ....$22.95

BEST OF SYSTEM OF A DOWN
00695788 ....$22.95

STEVE VAI
00673247 ....$22.95

STEVE VAI – ALIEN LOVE SECRETS: THE NAKED VAMPS
00695223 ....$22.95

STEVE VAI – FIRE GARDEN: THE NAKED VAMPS
00695166 ....$22.95

STEVE VAI – THE ULTRA ZONE: NAKED VAMPS
00695684 ....$22.95

STEVIE RAY VAUGHAN
00699316 ....$24.95

THE GUITAR STYLE OF STEVIE RAY VAUGHAN
00695155 ....$24.95

BEST OF THE VENTURES
00695772 ....$19.95

THE WHO
00695561 ....$22.95

BEST OF ZZ TOP
00695738 ....$22.95

Complete descriptions and songlists online!

FOR MORE INFORMATION, SEE YOUR LOCAL MUSIC DEALER, OR WRITE TO:

HAL•LEONARD®
CORPORATION
7777 W. BLUEMOUND RD. P.O. BOX 13819 MILWAUKEE, WI 53213

www.halleonard.com

Prices, contents and availability subject to change without notice.

0606

GUITAR RECORDED VERSIONS®

Guitar Recorded Versions® are note-for-note transcriptions of guitar music taken directly off recordings. This series, one of the most popular in print today, features some of the greatest guitar players and groups from blues and rock to country and jazz.

Guitar Recorded Versions are transcribed by the best transcribers in the business. Every book contains notes and tablature.

AUTHENTIC TRANSCRIPTIONS WITH NOTES AND TABLATURE

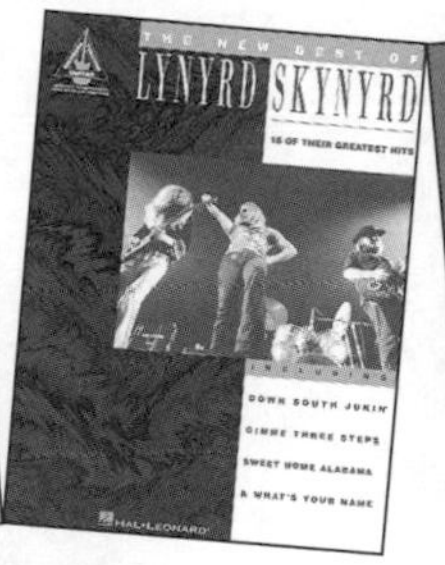

RECORDED VERSIONS GUITAR

AUTHENTIC TRANSCRIPTIONS WITH NOTES AND TABLATURE

00694757 Yngwie Malmsteen – Trilogy $19.95
00690754 Marilyn Manson – Lest We Forget $19.95
00694956 Bob Marley – Legend $19.95
00690075 Bob Marley – Natural Mystic $19.95
00690548 Very Best of Bob Marley & The Wailers – One Love $19.95
00694945 Bob Marley – Songs of Freedom $24.95
00690748 Maroon5 – 1.22.03 Acoustic $19.95
00690657 Maroon5 – Songs About Jane $19.95
00690442 Matchbox 20 – Mad Season $19.95
00690616 Matchbox 20 – More Than You Think You Are ..$19.95
00690239 Matchbox 20 – Yourself or Someone Like You ..$19.95
00690283 Best of Sarah McLachlan $19.95
00690382 Sarah McLachlan – Mirrorball $19.95
00690354 Sarah McLachlan – Surfacing $19.95
00120080 Don McLean Songbook $19.95
00694952 Megadeth – Countdown to Extinction $19.95
00690244 Megadeth – Cryptic Writings $19.95
00694951 Megadeth – Rust in Peace $22.95
00694953 Megadeth – Selections from Peace Sells...But Who's Buying? & So Far, So Good...So What! $22.95
00690768 Megadeth – The System Has Failed $19.95
00690495 Megadeth – The World Needs a Hero $19.95
00690011 Megadeth – Youthanasia $19.95
00690505 John Mellencamp Guitar Collection $19.95
00690562 Pat Metheny – Bright Size Life $19.95
00690646 Pat Metheny – One Quiet Night $19.95
00690559 Pat Metheny – Question & Answer $19.95
00690565 Pat Metheny – Rejoicing $19.95
00690558 Pat Metheny Trio – 99>00 ....$19.95
00690561 Pat Metheny Trio – Live $22.95
00690040 Steve Miller Band Greatest Hits $19.95
00690769 Modest Mouse – Good News for People Who Love Bad News $19.95
00694802 Gary Moore – Still Got the Blues $19.95
00690103 Alanis Morissette – Jagged Little Pill $19.95
00690786 Mudvayne – The End of All Things to Come $22.95
00690787 Mudvayne – L.D. 50 ....$22.95
00690794 Mudvayne – Lost and Found $19.95
00690448 MxPx – The Ever Passing Moment $19.95
00690500 Ricky Nelson Guitar Collection $17.95
00690722 New Found Glory – Catalyst $19.95
00690345 Best of Newsboys $17.95
00690611 Nirvana $22.95
00694895 Nirvana – Bleach $19.95
00690189 Nirvana – From the Muddy Banks of the Wishkah $19.95
00694913 Nirvana – In Utero $19.95
00694901 Nirvana – Incesticide $19.95
00694883 Nirvana – Nevermind $19.95
00690026 Nirvana – Unplugged in York $19.95
00690739 No Doubt – Rock Steady $22.95
00120112 No Doubt – Tragic Kingdom $22.95
00690273 Oasis – Be Here Now $19.95
00690159 Oasis – Definitely Maybe $19.95
00690121 Oasis – (What's the Story) Morning Glory $19.95
00690226 Oasis – The Other Side of Oasis $19.95
00690358 The Offspring – Americana $19.95
00690485 The Offspring – Conspiracy of One $19.95
00690807 The Offspring – Greatest Hits $19.95
00690204 The Offspring – Ixnay on the Hombre $17.95
00690203 The Offspring – Smash $18.95
00690663 The Offspring – Splinter $19.95
00694847 Best of Ozzy Osbourne $22.95
00694830 Ozzy Osbourne – No More Tears $19.95
00690399 Ozzy Osbourne – The Ozzman Cometh $19.95
00690129 Ozzy Osbourne – Ozzmosis $22.95
00690594 Best of Les Paul $19.95
00690546 P.O.D. – Satellite $19.95
00694855 Pearl Jam – Ten $19.95
00690439 A Perfect Circle – Mer De Noms $19.95
00690661 A Perfect Circle – Thirteenth Step $19.95
00690499 Tom Petty – Definitive Guitar Collection $19.95
00690176 Phish – Billy Breathes $22.95
00690424 Phish – Farmhouse $19.95
00690240 Phish – Hoist $19.95
00690331 Phish – Story of the Ghost $19.95
00690642 Pillar – Fireproof $19.95
00690731 Pillar – Where Do We Go from Here $19.95
00690428 Pink Floyd – Dark Side of the Moon $19.95
00693864 Best of The Police $19.95
00690299 Best of Elvis: The King of Rock 'n' Roll $19.95
00692535 Elvis Presley $18.95
00690003 Classic Queen $24.95
00694975 Queen – Greatest Hits $24.95
00690670 Very Best of Queensryche $19.95
00694910 Rage Against the Machine $19.95
00690145 Rage Against the Machine – Evil Empire $19.95
00690179 Rancid – And Out Come the Wolves $22.95
00690426 Best of Ratt $19.95
00690055 Red Hot Chili Peppers – Bloodsugarsexmagik ..$19.95
00690584 Red Hot Chili Peppers – By the Way $19.95
00690379 Red Hot Chili Peppers – Californication $19.95
00690673 Red Hot Chili Peppers – Greatest Hits $19.95
00690255 Red Hot Chili Peppers – Mother's Milk $19.95
00690090 Red Hot Chili Peppers – One Hot Minute $22.95
00690511 Django Reinhardt – The Definitive Collection $19.95
00690779 Relient K – MMHMM $19.95
00690643 Relient K – Two Lefts Don't Make a Right ... But Three Do $19.95
00694899 R.E.M. – Automatic for the People $19.95
00690260 Jimmie Rodgers Guitar Collection $19.95
00690014 Rolling Stones – Exile on Main Street $24.95
00690631 Rolling Stones – Guitar Anthology $24.95
00690186 Rolling Stones – Rock & Roll Circus $19.95
00690685 David Lee Roth – Eat 'Em and Smile $19.95
00690694 David Lee Roth – Guitar Anthology $24.95
00690749 Saliva – Survival of the Sickest $19.95
00690031 Santana's Greatest Hits $19.95
00690796 Very Best of Michael Schenker $19.95
00690566 Best of Scorpions $19.95
00690604 Bob Seger – Guitar Anthology $19.95
00690659 Bob Seger and the Silver Bullet Band – Greatest Hits, Volume 2 ....$17.95
00120105 Kenny Wayne Shepherd – Ledbetter Heights $19.95
00690750 Kenny Wayne Shepherd – The Place You're In ..$19.95
00120123 Kenny Wayne Shepherd – Trouble Is $19.95
00690196 Silverchair – Freak Show $19.95
00690130 Silverchair – Frogstomp $19.95
00690357 Silverchair – Neon Ballroom $19.95
00690419 Slipknot $19.95
00690530 Slipknot – Iowa $19.95
00690733 Slipknot – Volume 3 (The Subliminal Verses) ..$19.95
00690691 Smashing Pumpkins Anthology $19.95
00690330 Social Distortion – Live at the Roxy $19.95
00120004 Best of Steely Dan $24.95
00694921 Best of Steppenwolf $22.95
00690655 Best of Mike Stern $19.95
00694801 Best of Rod Stewart $22.95
00694957 Rod Stewart – Unplugged...And Seated $22.95
00690021 Sting – Fields of Gold $19.95
00694955 Sting for Guitar Tab $19.95
00690597 Stone Sour $19.95
00690689 Story of the Year – Page Avenue $19.95
00690520 Styx Guitar Collection $19.95
00120081 Sublime $19.95
00690519 SUM 41 – All Killer No Filler $19.95
00690771 SUM 41 – Chuck $19.95
00690612 SUM 41 – Does This Look Infected? $19.95
00690767 Switchfoot – The Beautiful Letdown $19.95
00690815 Switchfoot – Nothing Is Sound $19.95
00690425 System of a Down $19.95
00690799 System of a Down – Mezmerize $19.95
00690606 System of a Down – Steal This Album $19.95
00690531 System of a Down – Toxicity $19.95
00694824 Best of James Taylor $16.95
00694887 Best of Thin Lizzy $19.95
00690238 Third Eye Blind $19.95
00690671 Three Days Grace $19.95
00690738 3 Doors Down – Away from the Sun $22.95
00690737 3 Doors Down – The Better Life $22.95
00690776 3 Doors Down – Seventeen Days $19.95
00690267 311 ....$19.95
00690580 311 – From Chaos $19.95
00690269 311 – Grass Roots $19.95
00690268 311 – Music $19.95
00690665 Thursday – War All the Time $19.95
00690030 Toad the Wet Sprocket $19.95
00690654 Best of Train $19.95
00690233 Merle Travis Collection $19.95
00690683 Robin Trower – Bridge of Sighs $19.95
00690740 Shania Twain – Guitar Collection $19.95
00699191 U2 – Best of: 1980-1990 ....$19.95
00690732 U2 – Best of: 1990-2000 ....$19.95
00690775 U2 – How to Dismantle an Atomic Bomb $22.95
00694411 U2 – The Joshua Tree $19.95
00690039 Steve Vai – Alien Love Secrets $24.95
00690172 Steve Vai – Fire Garden $24.95
00690343 Steve Vai – Flex-able Leftovers $19.95
00660137 Steve Vai – Passion & Warfare $24.95
00690605 Steve Vai – Selections from the Elusive Light and Sound, Volume 1 ....$24.95
00694904 Steve Vai – Sex and Religion $24.95
00690392 Steve Vai – The Ultra Zone $22.95
00690023 Jimmie Vaughan – Strange Pleasures $19.95
00690455 Stevie Ray Vaughan – Blues at Sunrise $19.95
00690024 Stevie Ray Vaughan – Couldn't Stand the Weather ..$19.95
00690370 Stevie Ray Vaughan and Double Trouble – The Real Deal: Greatest Hits Volume 2 ....$22.95
00690116 Stevie Ray Vaughan – Guitar Collection $24.95
00660136 Stevie Ray Vaughan – In Step $19.95
00694879 Stevie Ray Vaughan – In the Beginning $19.95
00660058 Stevie Ray Vaughan – Lightnin' Blues '83-'87 ....$24.95
00690036 Stevie Ray Vaughan – Live Alive $24.95
00690417 Stevie Ray Vaughan – Live at Carnegie Hall $19.95
00690550 Stevie Ray Vaughan and Double Trouble – Live at Montreux 1982 & 1985 ....$24.95
00694835 Stevie Ray Vaughan – The Sky Is Crying $22.95
00690025 Stevie Ray Vaughan – Soul to Soul $19.95
00690015 Stevie Ray Vaughan – Texas Flood $19.95
00694776 Vaughan Brothers – Family Style $19.95
00690772 Velvet Revolver – Contraband $19.95
00690132 The T-Bone Walker Collection $19.95
00694789 Muddy Waters – Deep Blues $24.95
00690071 Weezer (The Blue Album) $19.95
00690516 Weezer (The Green Album) $19.95
00690800 Weezer – Make Believe $19.95
00690286 Weezer – Pinkerton $19.95
00690447 Best of The Who $24.95
00694970 The Who – Definitive Guitar Collection: A-E $24.95
00694971 The Who – Definitive Guitar Collection: F-Li $24.95
00694972 The Who – Definitive Guitar Collection: Lo-R $24.95
00694973 The Who – Definitive Guitar Collection: S-Y $24.95
00690640 David Wilcox – Anthology 2000-2003 ....$19.95
00690325 David Wilcox – Collection $17.95
00690672 Best of Dar Williams $19.95
00690320 Dar Williams Songbook $17.95
00690319 Stevie Wonder – Some of the Best $17.95
00690596 Best of the Yardbirds $19.95
00690710 Yellowcard – Ocean Avenue $19.95
00690507 Frank Zappa – Apostrophe $19.95
00690443 Frank Zappa – Hot Rats $19.95
00690589 ZZ Top – Guitar Anthology $22.95

THE DECADE SERIES

These Guitar Recorded Versions collections feature the top tunes that shaped a decade, transcribed note-for-note with tab.

The 1950s

35 pivotal songs from the early rock years: All Shook Up • Donna • Heartbreak Hotel • Hound Dog • I'm Movin' On • Lonesome Town • Matchbox • Moonlight in Vermont • My Babe • Poor Little Fool • Race With the Devil • Rebel 'Rouser • Rock Around the Clock • Rockin' Robin • Sleepwalk • Slippin' and Slidin' • Sweet Little Angel • Tequila • Wake Up Little Susie • Yankee Doodle Dixie • and more.

00690543.................................$15.95

The 1960s

30 songs that defined the '60s: Badge • Blackbird • Fun, Fun, Fun • Gloria • Good Lovin' • Happy Together • Hey Joe • Hush • I Can See for Miles • I Feel Fine • I Get Around • Louie, Louie • My Girl • Oh, Pretty Woman • On the Road Again • Somebody to Love • Soul Man • Suite: Judy Blue Eyes • Susie-Q • Wild Thing • and more.

00690542.................................$15.95

The 1970s

30 top songs from the '70s: Best of My Love • Breakdown • Dust in the Wind • Evil Woman • Landslide • Lay Down Sally • Let It Be • Maggie May • No Woman No Cry • Oye Como Va • Show Me the Way • Smoke on the Water • So Into You • Space Oddity • Stayin' Alive • Teach Your Children • Time in a Bottle • Walk This Way • Wheel in the Sky • You've Got a Friend • and more.

00690541.................................$16.95

The 1980s

30 songs that best represent the decade: 867-5309/Jenny • Every Breath You Take • Eye of the Tiger • Fight for Your Right (To Party) • Heart and Soul • Hit Me With Your Best Shot • I Love Rock 'N Roll • La Bamba • Money for Nothing • Mony, Mony • Refugee • Rock Me • Rock You Like a Hurricane • Start Me Up • Summer of '69 • Sweet Child O' Mine • Wait • What I Like About You • and more.

00690540.................................$16.95

The 1990s

30 essential '90s classics: All I Wanna Do • Barely Breathing • Building a Mystery • Come Out and Play • Cryin' • Fields of Gold • Friends in Low Places • Hold My Hand • I Can't Dance • Iris • Jump, Jive an' Wail • More Than Words • Santa Monica • Semi-Charmed Life • Silent Lucidity • Smells Like Teen Spirit • Smooth • Tears in Heaven • Two Princes • Under the Bridge • Wonderwall • and more.

00690539.................................$16.95

The 2000s

30 songs, including: Alive • All the Small Things • Are You Gonna Be My Girl • Californication • Click Click Boom • Complicated • Drive • Hanging by a Moment • Heaven • If You're Gone • Kryptonite • Lifestyles of the Rich and Famous • Maps • The Space Between • Take a Look Around (Theme from *M:I-2*) • Wherever You Will Go • Yellow • and more.

00690761.................................$15.95

More of the 1950s

30 top songs of the '50s, including: Blue Suede Shoes • Bye Bye Love • Don't Be Cruel (To a Heart That's True) • Hard Headed Woman • Jailhouse Rock • La Bamba • Peggy Sue • Rawhide • Say Man • See You Later, Alligator • That'll Be the Day • Yakety Yak • and more.

00690756.................................$14.95

More of the 1960s

30 great songs of the '60s: All Along the Watchtower • Born to Be Wild • Brown Eyed Girl • California Dreamin' • Do You Believe in Magic • Hang On Sloopy • I'm a Believer • Paperback Writer • Secret Agent Man • So You Want to Be a Rock and Roll Star • Sunshine of Your Love • Surfin' U.S.A. • Ticket to Ride • Travelin' Man • White Rabbit • With a Little Help from My Friends • and more.

00690757.................................$14.95

More of the 1970s

30 more hits from the '70s: Aqualung • Carry on Wayward Son • Evil Ways • Feel like Makin' Love • Fly like an Eagle • Give a Little Bit • I Want You to Want Me • Lights • My Sharona • One Way or Another • Rock and Roll All Nite • Roxanne • Saturday Night's Alright (For Fighting) • Suffragette City • Sultans of Swing • Sweet Emotion • Sweet Home Alabama • Won't Get Fooled Again • Wonderful Tonight • and more.

00690758.................................$17.95

More of the 1980s

30 songs that defined the decade: Call Me • Crazy Crazy Nights • Heartbreaker • Here I Go Again • It's Still Rock and Roll to Me • Jack and Diane • Jessie's Girl • Once Bitten Twice Shy • Rock the Casbah • Runnin' Down a Dream • Sharp Dressed Man • Smokin' in the Boys Room • Stray Cat Strut • Wanted Dead or Alive • White Wedding • and more.

00690759.................................$16.95

More of the 1990s

30 songs: Alive • Change the World • Come as You Are • The Freshmen • Hard to Handle • Hole Hearted • Just a Girl • Lightning Crashes • Mr. Jones • No Excuses • No Rain • Only Wanna Be with You • Pretty Fly (For a White Guy) • Push • Shimmer • Stay • Stupid Girl • What I Got • Whatever • Whiskey in the Jar • Zombie • and more.

00690760.................................$14.95

More of the 2000s

30 recent hits: All Downhill From Here • By the Way • Clocks • Cold Hard Bitch • Drops of Jupiter (Tell Me) • Harder to Breathe • I Did It • I Hate Everything About You • Learn to Fly • Ocean Avenue • St. Anger • Wasting My Time • When I'm Gone • Wish You Were Here • With Arms Wide Open • Youth of the Nation • and more.

00690762.................................$16.95

Prices, contents and availability subject to change without notice.

FOR MORE INFORMATION, SEE YOUR LOCAL MUSIC DEALER, OR WRITE TO:

HAL•LEONARD® CORPORATION

7777 W. BLUEMOUND RD. P.O. BOX 13819 MILWAUKEE, WI 53213

Complete songlists available online at
www.halleonard.com

0706